THE GENTLE ART OF VERBAL SELF-DEFENSE

Suzette Haden Elgin

THE GENTLE ART OF VERBAL SELF-DEFENSE

BARNES
& NOBLE
BOOKS
NEW YORK

This edition published by Barnes & Noble, Inc.,
by arrangement with Suzette Haden Elgin.

1993 Barnes & Noble Books

ISBN 0-88029-030-7 *casebound*
ISBN 0-88029-257-1 *paperback*

Printed and bound in the United States of America

MC 41 40 39 38 37 36
MP 12 11 10 9 8 7 6 5

Contents

ACKNOWLEDGMENTS

My grateful thanks go to Virginia Satir, to John Grinder, to Richard Bandler, and to the many other scholars and researchers whose work laid the foundations upon which mine is based; and to the many people who have offered comments and suggestions in my classes and workshops over the years. It would also be appropriate for me to give a large measure of credit at this point to those individuals who have offered me the opportunity to hone my personal skills in verbal self-defense.

Suzette Haden Elgin

ACKNOWLEDGMENTS

[illegible]

[illegible]

Introduction

The Four Basic Principles

1

For every person in this society who is suffering physical abuse, there are hundreds suffering the effects of verbal violence. For every person who just got a fist in the face, there are hundreds who just took a verbal blow to the gut. And there are major differences between these two kinds of injury.

The physical attack is at least obvious and unmistakable; when someone slugs you physically, you can call the police. The physical attack hurts horribly and leaves a mark, but it is usually over fast, and the mark is evidence in your favor and against your attacker.

Verbal violence is a very different matter. Except in

rare cases—for example, when someone lies about you publicly before witnesses and can be charged with slander—there is no agency that you can call for help. The pain of verbal abuse goes deep into the self and festers there, but because nothing shows on the surface, it will not win you even sympathy, much less actual assistance.

Worst of all, verbal violence all too often goes unrecognized, except at a level that you cannot even understand yourself. You know that you are suffering, and you vaguely know where the pain is coming from; but because the aggression is so well hidden, you are likely to blame yourself instead of the aggressor, and to add to your own misery, like this:

> "I can't understand why I feel so *stupid* when I'm with her. She's always so considerate and she's such a nice person! There must be something the matter with *me*."

There probably is something the matter with you, yes. Your problem is that you are the victim of verbal violence and you don't have the least idea how to defend yourself against it. When someone looks you right in the eye and says, "You're an idiot!" you know that's verbal abuse and you probably have ways of dealing with it. But when someone smiles at you and says, "Even *you* should be able to understand why that won't work!" it's not so easy—especially if a few "sweethearts" or "old pals" or "darlings" are scattered around to confuse you.

We get little or no training in verbal self-defense. Once upon a time anyone who pretended to an education learned it. It was called rhetoric, and if we really went back to the "basics," we would have to put it back in our curriculum. (Today a "rhetoric class" usually means a course in writing compositions.) Informal training outside the school system is given to most men, but not in adequate measure; women receive no instruction at all, formal or informal. This is a gap that needs filling.

This book is a manual to teach you verbal judo. Unlike a number of books now available, it is not intended to train you to attack others or to be violent yourself. Instead you will learn how to use your opponent's strength and momentum as tools for your own defense. You will learn to head off verbal confrontation so skillfully that it rarely happens, and to do so with honor. The person with a black belt in a martial art is not likely to be a violent person. Knowing that you are fully capable not only of defending yourself adequately but also of inflicting harm on others makes you a very careful person. Far more careful than you would be if you reacted to every threatening situation with an untrained panic response.

There are four basic principles of verbal self-defense that you must master.

FIRST PRINCIPLE

Know that you are under attack.

You must be able to recognize a situation in which you are in danger or actually under attack. If you continually assume that the reason you come out of conversations feeling somehow hurt and depressed is that you are "oversensitive" or "paranoid" or "childish," you will not recognize danger when it exists. If you can always be taken by surprise because you have no idea what verbal aggression is or how to spot it, you are an ideal target. The vast majority of verbal attacks will not even take place if you are trained in verbal self-defense.

Just as the hoodlum planning a mugging is likely to back off and change plans at the discovery that the victim is not helpless, so will the verbal mugger look for someone who is not going to be able or willing to fight back. You must learn to recognize the signs of verbal violence. You must become so aware of them that you can sense the most subtle indications, often before *any* words are spoken aloud.

SECOND PRINCIPLE

Know what kind of attack you are facing.

You must learn to judge and recognize your opponent's weapon(s), strength, and skill. Obvious characteristics—such as the loudness of someone's voice or an unpleasant facial expression or the use of openly insulting (or openly flattering!) words—are not reliable indicators of these things. Often a reliance on the "obvious" signs will mislead you completely and leave you defenseless.

THIRD PRINCIPLE

Know how to make your defense fit the attack.

The response you make must match your opponent's move. You must choose an appropriate response and an appropriate level of intensity. Not only is there no need for you to waste your energy on a weak opponent with little skill, it is unethical and cowardly for you to do so. You don't go after bunny rabbits with an elephant gun. And just as it would be foolish to choose a sword as a weapon against someone armed with a machine gun, the verbal weapon should be chosen to fit the occasion. The phrase "Enough is enough" is not a cliché in the art of verbal self-defense. On the contrary, there is no excuse for anything more than just exactly enough.

FOURTH PRINCIPLE

Know how to follow through.

You must be able to carry out your response once you have chosen it. For many people, and perhaps especially for women, this may be the most difficult part of verbal self-defense. It is a source of astonishment to many a policeman to find that the victim of a physical assault in a marriage is a woman who is actually larger and stronger than the man. Nevertheless, there are strong cultural pressures against a woman's using violence at all. Many women cannot bring themselves to do it, even when it is entirely justified. The same problem exists when your opponent is, in physical terms, smaller or weaker than you are, no matter what your sex. We have all been taught to "pick on somebody our own size." In verbal confrontations it may be difficult to remember that size has nothing whatever to do with strength and that some of the most skilled of verbal bullies are only six years old.

It will help if you keep in mind that verbal self-defense is a *gentle* art. It is a way of *preventing* violence. When a parent picks up a small child who is just about to whack a playmate over the head with a toy truck, that act is interfering with the child's freedom and is, in a formal sense, a kind of violence. (Especially if, as is often true, the child must be physically restrained from carrying out his or her plans.) Verbal self-defense is like that; except in the most extreme cases, if skillfully used, it is a nonviolent activity and a way of keeping the peace without resorting to force.

If the Fourth Principle is a problem for you, you had better be prepared to feel and to work through a certain amount of guilt. You will be attacked; you will use the techniques in this book to defend yourself against your attacker; and then you will feel guilty. Later we will take up ways of handling this, but for now just accept the fact that it *will* happen. Healthy people don't enjoy causing other people pain, even when it is well and thoroughly deserved.

The Five Satir Modes

2

In order to learn any new skill you need a set of words, a vocabulary for discussing it. In verbal self-defense much of that vocabulary has already been provided in a different context and can now be adapted to our use.

Virginia Satir is one of the foremost therapists in the United States and is famous all over the world for her work in family and other types of therapy. In her books she has developed a set of terms for common verbal behavior patterns. There are five such patterns in her system; we will be calling them the Satir Modes.* This book is not about therapy, but the terms are just what we need to serve as our working vocabulary. They are:

THE PLACATER

The Placater is frightened that other people will become angry, go away, and never come back again. The Placater doesn't dare admit this, however. Typical Placater speech:

- "Oh, you know me—*I* don't care!"
- "Whatever anybody else wants to do is fine with me."
- "Whatever you say, darling; I don't mind."
- "Oh, nothing bothers me! Do whatever you like."
- "What do I want to do? Oh, I don't know—what would *you* like to do?"

Caution: It often happens in my work that everyone assumes all Placaters are female. (The women present are as given to this as the men.) It isn't so; try listening carefully to some men and you'll find that out in a hurry.

Few conversations are as dead-end and hopeless as two Placaters trying to reach a decision, with a dialogue like this one:

A: Where shall we go for dinner?

B: I don't know. Where would you like to go?

A: Oh, *you* pick. *You* know me, *I* don't care where we go.

B: No, really, *you* decide!

A: But it doesn't matter to me at all!

B: It doesn't matter to me, either, you know that.

*The Satir Modes were further developed by John Grinder and Richard Bandler, who are also therapists, as well as by the associates who have joined them as their work progressed. They then analyzed the modes for use in various kinds of therapy. If you are interested in exploring this, please refer to the list of references and suggested readings.

A: Seriously, I'd much much rather *you* . . .
(and so on forever)

Whenever you hear anyone referred to as "Good Old" So-and-So, there is at least a fifty-fifty chance that Good Old X is a Placater.

THE BLAMER

The Blamer feels that nobody cares about him or her, that there is no respect or affection for him, and that people are all indifferent to his needs and feelings. The Blamer reacts to this with a verbal behavior pattern intended to demonstrate that he or she is in charge, is the boss, is the one with power. Typical Blamer speech:

- "You never consider my feelings."
- "Nobody around here ever pays any attention to me."
- "Do you *always* have to put yourself first?"
- "Why don't you ever think about what *I* might want? I've had all of this I'm going to take!"
- "Why do you always insist on having your own way, no matter how much it hurts other people?"

When two Blamers talk to each other, the conversation is not a dead end, as it is with two Placaters. It is a broad and rapid road to a screaming match, nasty in every way.

THE COMPUTER

The Computer is terrified that someone will find out what his or her feelings are. If possible, the Computer will give the impression that he *has* no feelings. *Star Trek's* Mr. Spock was—except for the troublesome human side of him that made him so interesting—an excellent example of a Computer. Computers talk like this:

- "There is undoubtedly a simple solution to the problem."
- "It's obvious that no real difficulty exists here."

- "No rational person would be alarmed by this crisis."
- "Clearly the advantages of this activity have been exaggerated."
- "Preferences of the kind you describe are rather common in this area."

Computers work hard at never saying "I" unless they qualify it heavily, as in "I suppose it is at least possible that . . ." And they use an extraordinarily limited set of facial expressions and body positions.

THE DISTRACTER

The Distracter is a tricky one to keep up with, because he or she does not hold to any of the previous patterns. Instead, the Distracter cycles rapidly among the other patterns, continually shifting Satir Modes. The underlying feeling of the Distracter is panic: "I don't know what on earth to say, but I've got to say SOMETHING, and the quicker the better!" The surface behavior will be a chaotic mix.

THE LEVELER

The Leveler is the most contradictory type of all—either the easiest or the most difficult to handle. The Leveler does just what Dr. Satir's term implies; this person levels with you. When the Leveler is genuine, there is nothing simpler to deal with—just level back. A *phony* Leveler, however, is more dangerous than all the other categories combined, and very hard to spot. If we assume that we are discussing the genuine article, what the Leveler says is what the Leveler feels.

If we had five terrified people trapped in an elevator that had stopped between floors, one from each of the Satir Modes, their remarks as the elevator hung there would be something like this:

Placater: Oh, I *hope* I didn't do anything to cause this. I sure didn't *mean* to!

Blamer: Which one of you idiots was fooling around with the buttons?

Computer: There is undoubtedly some perfectly simple reason why this elevator isn't moving. Certainly there is no cause whatever for alarm.

Distracter: Did one of you hit the Stop button? Oh, I didn't *mean* that; of course none of you would do anything like that! It is, however, extremely easy to do that sort of thing by accident. *Why* do things like this only happen to me?

Leveler: Personally, I'm scared.

You will notice one thing about the descriptions of these verbal behavior patterns. In every one of them, except for the Leveler, there is a strong clash between the inner feelings and the outer verbal behavior. When someone is locked into one of these modes and cannot communicate effectively in any other way, he or she may be in emotional difficulty—again, except for the Leveler. The Leveler is not having trouble communicating.

Although most people seem to have a *preferred* Satir Mode under stress, they are not confined to it. And they can choose, either deliberately or unconsciously, to use any one of the modes at will, as the situation demands. In this case—that is, when the communicator is in control of the pattern used—the classic mismatch between inside and outside may not exist at all. A person may decide to use Computer Mode because he or she is in a committee meeting and it seems appropriate; the choice does not necessarily indicate that such a person is afraid others will suspect his or her underlying emotions. A parent who feels perfectly secure in a position of dominance over a child may choose Blamer Mode deliberately as a way of disciplining that child.

In this book we will not be concerned with the situation in which an individual has no choice as to which mode will be used. That is properly left to the expert therapist. We can, however, adapt the category names to the art of verbal self-defense, since they appear to represent the most common types of verbal aggression. Like the sword, the gun, the stick, and the hatpin, the Satir Modes are both weapons of verbal conflict and mechanisms for forestalling such conflict. You must learn to recognize them and to use them with confidence and skill.

It's important for you to remember that a true Leveler is not likely to be attacking you, in spite of the surface indicators. For example:

> *Leveler:* You know, you drive me crazy tapping your ballpoint pen on the desk like that. It really bothers me.

This is not an attack, it's a simple statement of fact and an invitation for an equally level response. For example:

> *You:* I know what you mean. It would drive me crazy, too. What's even worse is somebody who whistles under his breath all the time.
>
> *Leveler:* Right. That's worse. I'd just as soon you didn't do either one.
>
> *You:* I'll try. Okay?
>
> *Leveler:* Fair enough.

That is not fighting, it's negotiation. It's very easy to turn it *into* a fight, however. One of the ironies of verbal interaction is that so many people mistake the statements of the Leveler for verbal violence and never suspect that the nice guy (or the nice lady) down the hall is the one who is really giving them a hard time.

Keep the Satir Modes in mind as we go along; they

are your basic inventory of *stances* for self-defense. Learn to spot them when they are coming at you; learn to use them consciously when they are needed and appropriate.

In an emergency, when you have no time to think or when you have not had sufficient training or practice to be sure of what you are doing, your safest "guess" stance is always Computer Mode. *Assume that stance and maintain it until you have a good reason to change.* Here is a preliminary summary of the characteristics of Computer Mode; we'll return to them again throughout the book.

THE COMPUTER . . .

- is never angry or emotional or hurried or upset.
- never talks in the first person singular ("I," "me," "my," "mine," "myself") without a heavy artillery of modifying sequences.
- always talks in abstractions and generalities.
- says, "It is _____ that . . . ;", for example, "It is obvious that there is no cause for alarm."
- says, "One would . . ." or "Any reasonable person would . . ."
- always *looks* absolutely calm and relaxed.
- usually takes a single physical position early in the conversation and maintains it from then on.
- never commits himself or herself to anything.

If you don't know what to do, the rule is always: SWITCH TO COMPUTER MODE AND STAY THERE. There is no safer stance.

REFERENCES AND SUGGESTED READINGS

GRINDER, JOHN, and RICHARD BANDLER. *The Structure of Magic:II*. Palo Alto, Calif.: Science and Behavior Books,

Inc., 1976. (For a discussion of the Satir Modes in therapy, see pp. 47–53.)

SATIR, VIRGINIA. *Conjoint Family Therapy.* Palo Alto, Calif.: Science and Behavior Books, Inc., 1964.

______. *Peoplemaking.* Palo Alto, Calif.: Science and Behavior Books, Inc., 1972.

Propositions of Power

The Verbal Violence Octagon

3

Another term that is needed in verbal self-defense is the "presupposition." It is a term used in a number of different ways by scholars in various fields. So that there will be no confusion, I am going to define it for this book as follows:

> A presupposition is something that a native speaker of a language knows is part of the meaning of a sequence of that language, even if it is not overtly present in the sequence.

For instance, every native speaker of English knows that the utterance "Even Bill could get an A in that class" means (a) that Bill is no great shakes as a student; and (b) that the class is not difficult in any way. But notice that *neither one* of those pieces of information is present in the surface structure of the sentence, in its overt wording. That is, the sentence does not read, "Even Bill, who is certainly no great shakes as a student, could get an A in that class, which is not difficult in any way." Nevertheless, that is what it *means*. The two extra pieces are said to be part of the presuppositions of the utterance.

A major reason why people do not realize that verbal violence is being used against them is that they have never been taught about presuppositions. They know about them, of course, below the level of conscious awareness. That's why they feel hurt or insulted in response to something that sounds, on the surface, like a nice thing to say. But they have never been taught to watch out for presuppositions, or to pay attention to them instead of the words that form the surface sequence. As a result, they cannot express *why* they feel hurt or insulted.

The illustration in figure 3–1 is a training device that we will be using in this book to make you aware of presuppositions. Although there are many other patterns of verbal violence, the eight shown on the Octagon are the most basic and the most common. In each section of the Octagon there is an utterance pattern in which a particular message can be hidden away as a *presupposition* of that utterance.

In this chapter we will go quickly through all eight sections of the Octagon; then, in the chapters following, we will take up each section in detail and consider strategies for dealing with it.

The most important principle at this stage of your training is to remember always to respond to the presupposition, *never* to the sequence it is hidden in. The steps of your strategy go like this:

The Verbal Violence Octagon:
Propositions of Power

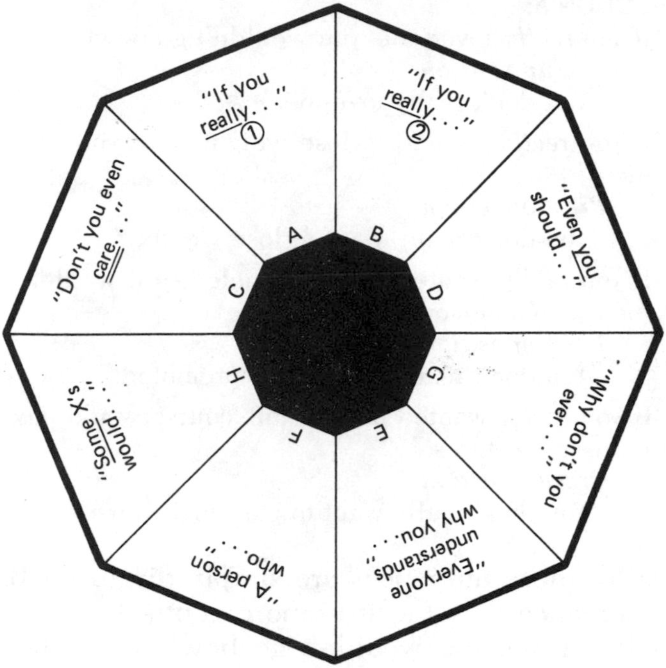

© Suzette Haden Elgin 1978

Figure 3—1

1. Identify the Satir Mode being used.
2. Identify the presupposition(s) of the sequence.
3. Respond in Computer Mode, with a neutral request for information about the presupposition or a remark about the presupposition.
4. Maintain Computer Mode.

Now let's go around the Verbal Violence Octagon briefly, one section at a time, with examples of typical utterances and their relevant presuppositions.

SECTION A:

- "If you *really* loved me, you wouldn't go bowling."
  Presupposition:
  "You don't really love me."
- "If you *really* wanted to lose weight, you wouldn't eat so much."
  Presupposition:
  "You don't really want to lose weight."
- "If you *really* wanted to be promoted, you wouldn't go to lunch with a person like that."
  Presupposition:
  "You don't really want to be promoted."
- "If you *really* wanted to pass this course, you'd pay attention to my lectures."
  Presupposition:
  "You don't really want to pass this course."

All of these utterances are simply disguised Blamer Mode sentences. It is a little more subtle to say "If you *really* loved me, you wouldn't go bowling," rather than "You don't care anything about me, and the way I can tell is because you go bowling," but the meaning is the same. In a Section A the flat Blamer Mode accusation is hidden away as the presupposition.

SECTION B:

- "If you really loved me, you wouldn't *want* to go bowling."
  Presuppositions:
  "You don't really love me."
  "You have the power to control your feelings if you want to."

Section B's are like a broadax dipped in poison. They are Section A attacks escalated to one more level of viciousness and are of course in Blamer Mode.

In the example sentence about going bowling given

under Section A, if you stop going bowling you have "proved" that you really do love the other person. But "If you really loved me, you wouldn't *want* to go bowling" traps you hopelessly. Whether you go bowling or not, you can't win—you are still going to *want* to go. And since you have swallowed the presupposition that if you really loved this person you wouldn't want to go, you are going to feel guilty no matter what you do. If you go bowling, you'll feel guilty because you're going; if you don't go, you'll feel guilty because you wish you had. The fact that somebody begins this sequence with "Sweetheart" does not turn it into a loving, tender thing to say. When you hear it, you've been slugged. Learn to recognize that.

SECTION C:

- "Don't you even *care* about your children?"

  Presuppositions:

  "You don't care about your children."

  "You *should* care about your children; it's wrong of you not to."

  "Therefore, you should feel rotten."
- "Don't you even *care* about your appearance?"
- "Don't you even *care* what happens to the other students?"
- "Don't you even *care* what the neighbors will say to your mother?"

Section C's are a fairly straightforward Blamer Mode, even on the surface. It's hard to imagine one of these sounding like anything except an accusation.

Notice that the word "care" is heavily stressed in these examples. That's important. It's one way for you to tell the difference between a genuinely interested request for information, such as might come from a Leveler who simply wanted to know, and a verbal attack. The presence of our old friend "even" is also a clue.

Take that last example. If it comes from a Leveler, someone who has no violence in mind, it is far more likely to take this form:

> "Don't you care what the neighbors will say to your mother?"

There is no stress on the word "care," and no "even" in the sentence; the intonation (the melody of the utterance) is quite different.

SECTION D:

- "Even an *elderly* person should be able to understand this rule." (There's "even" again—watch it!)

  Presuppositions:

  "There's something wrong with being an elderly person."

  "It doesn't take much intelligence or ability to understand this rule."

  "You should feel guilty and stupid."
- "Even a *woman* should be able to grasp basic economics."
- "Even a *freshman* ought to be able to pass this test."
- "Even the *second*-graders know how to do *that*."

And, for primitive whacking and slashing . . .

- "Even *you* should be able to follow this argument."

. . . which presupposes that there is something terribly wrong with simply being you.

You will notice that it's possible to pile these up into multiples. For instance:

> "Even a woman who doesn't even *care* about her appearance should be able to understand that plaids are not becoming except on thin people."

This is brutal; go to Computer Mode and maintain it.

The Section D attacks are in a mild Computer Mode, as are all of the presuppositions except the final accusing one. It is an abstract reference to a class of individuals, with the same surface form as a statement like "Even water in excess can be poisonous."

SECTION E:

- "Everyone understands why you are having such a hard time adjusting to this job."

  Presuppositions:

  "You are having a hard time adjusting to this job."

  "Everybody knows about the problem you have that's *causing* your difficulty in adjustment, so there's no point trying to hide or deny it."
- "Everyone understands why you are so emotional these days, darling."
- "Everyone understands perfectly why you are becoming hysterical, Mrs. Smith."

This particular type of attack sounds so much like Leveler Mode that it can catch you off your guard. The presence of that all-knowing and unidentified "everyone" at the beginning should be a warning; this is a Computer talking, usually with a Blamer windup. Because it is so carefully orchestrated, however, it is nothing like the Distracter Mode. Distracter Mode *has* no pattern for you to observe.

SECTION F:

- "A person who really wanted to succeed wouldn't object to a trivial regulation like our dress code."

  Presupposition:

  "You don't really want to succeed."
- "A person who has serious emotional problems can't be

expected to cope with the work load here like the other employees do, Mr. Rohr."

Presuppositions:
"You have serious emotional problems."
"The work load here is reasonable for an individual who does not have serious emotional problems."

- "A boy who *really* wanted people to know he wasn't a sissy wouldn't sit around reading all the time."

  Presuppositions:
  "You really want people to think you're a sissy."
  "Sissies sit around reading all the time . . . like you do."

Section F's are basically Computer Mode.

SECTION G:

- "Why don't you ever want me to be happy?"

  Presuppositions:
  "You don't want me to be happy."
  "You have the power to make me happy, if only you were willing to use it."

Sometimes this turns up in a flipped form: "Why do you always want me to be miserable?", but this is a valuable clue to the amount of danger you are in. Your opponent doesn't have much skill if he or she leaves anything so obvious dangling out in the open like that.

- "Why don't you ever act like other mothers?"
- "Why don't you ever take a close look at yourself?"
- "Why don't you ever think about the welfare of the other students in this class?"
- "Why don't you ever consider the feelings of *other* people?"

No amount of tinkering will make "Why don't you ever"

different enough from "You never" to remove it from Blamer Mode.

SECTION H:

- "*Some* husbands would object to having their wives go back to school when the kids are still just babies."

    Presuppositions:

    "It's wrong for you to go back to school."

    "I'm not like other husbands—I'm unique and superior to them because I'm not objecting to your going back to school."

    "I have the power to let you go back to school or not, just as I like."

    "You should feel very guilty about going back to school."

    "You should feel *very* grateful to me."

All this, and Computer Mode as well? That's right. Although the entire set of presuppositions is in Blamer Mode, not to mention all those claims about "I" and the powers that "I" has, the surface form is Computer Mode. Here are a few more examples of this attack, which is definitely the most advanced on the Octagon:

- "*Some* bosses would object to having an employee who always leaves work five minutes early to catch a bus."
- "*Some* professors would really be upset about getting a term paper that wasn't even typed."
- "*Some* wives would really get mad if their husbands went fishing over the weekend and left them at home alone."
- "*Some* landlords would seriously consider taking action if they had a tenant who never made any attempt to take care of his apartment."

By no means does this cover all of the possible stances of verbal violence. But because most people are no better trained in the art of verbal self-defense than you are, you aren't likely to encounter many techniques that are anything more than a variation of these eight basic ones.

If you can defend yourself against the eight moves on the Octagon, your skills will develop and lead you on from that level to more advanced techniques. In verbal self-defense, as in any other art, if you master the basics and apply them by frequent practice, you are well on your way.

HOW TO USE THE NEXT EIGHT CHAPTERS

Now we are going to move on and take up each Octagon Section in detail, one to a chapter. The chapters are carefully designed for your self-training.

At the beginning of each chapter you will find an octagon like figure 3–1, except that its sections are left blank. As you read the chapter, you will think of examples from your personal life that you want to analyze. If you don't make a note of these, they will slip your mind, and then when you are free to work on them, you won't be able to recall what they were. To avoid this, write them down in the sections of the blank octagon as they occur to you.

You'll also find in each of the next eight chapters a Journal section in which you can record verbal confrontations from your own life—both what was actually said and what *ought* to have been said. At first you will be much better at working these out after they are over, when it is too late, than you are when they are actually going on. For that purpose the Journal is invaluable. You can try as many different versions of the way it should have gone as you like, with no additional penalties. And you should of course feel free to supplement the space provided in this manual with as many additional pages of your own as you feel you need. The later chapters are more difficult than the early ones; as in any martial art, you will progress from the simpler moves to the more complex ones, increasing your skill as you go. You may find, therefore, that the later chapters seem to require a lot more Journal space than the economics of book publishing will allow, in which case you should add that space. There is no way to predict for every individual just what the perfect amount of Journal pages and lines would be in any section, since that will depend upon your personal life.

Finally, each of these chapters contains sample verbal confrontations in which some lines have been left blank for you to fill in. Then, at the end of the chapter, you will find four possible ways that the confrontation could have been worked out, with an analysis of the verbal moves. When you have filled in the example, you should compare your solution with the end-of-chapter suggestions, remembering that there will always be many possible "correct" answers.

Now let's begin.

SUGGESTED READINGS

Book:

LE GUIN, URSULA K. *The Wind's Twelve Quarters*. New York: Bantam Books, Inc., 1976. (See pp. 244–50, "Direction of the Road," a brief short story that illustrates how much we take our presuppositions for granted—from an unusual point of view.)

Articles:

BOHANNON, LAURA. "Shakespeare in the Bush," *Natural History,* August–September 1966, pp. 28–33. (This article is a fine demonstration of the astonishing differences of meaning that can occur when speakers do not share the same basic presuppositions.)

MORAN, TERENCE P. "Public Doublespeak: 1984 and Beyond," *College English* 37, no. 2 (October 1975): 200–222.

Section A Attacks

If You *Really* . . . (I)

4

This section is one of the most elementary verbal attack patterns and is an excellent place for the novice to begin practice. The surface structure for a Section A move looks like this:

> If you *really* (X), you would/wouldn't (Y).

The X's and Y's may be filled by almost anything, depending on the situation, but the verbal frame into which they fit will be as shown. Any utterance coming at you in this form should immediately alert you to the possibility that you are headed for a verbal confrontation.

Your Personal Octagon

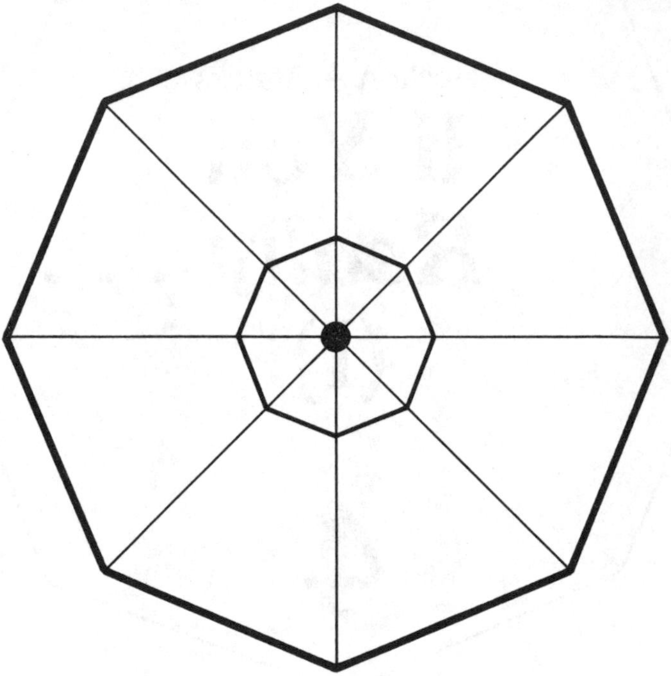

© Suzette Haden Elgin 1978

The stronger the stress placed on the word "really," the more likely it is that you are under attack. The presupposition that matters is, of course, "You don't really (X)." and what is crucial is that you recognize the presupposition and respond to *it*, not to the content of (Y). Whatever fills (Y) is only the bait, the element your opponent is using to distract you; and ordinarily the move is successful. That is, the person who neither realizes that an attack is under way nor knows how to handle it takes the bait and responds to (Y). This is a sure way to lose the confrontation. Let's look at a very simple, and very common, example.

CONFRONTATION ONE

Man: If you *really* loved me, you wouldn't waste so much money.

Woman: I *don't* waste money! Do you have any idea what it *costs* to feed a family these days?

(WOMAN has already lost this one, no matter what happens from this point on, because she has completely ignored MAN'S real challenge—that she doesn't love him. By not responding to that challenge, hidden in the presuppositions, she has conceded the point and admitted by default that he is right. But let's look at a few more moves nonetheless.)

Man: I notice that your sister manages to feed *her* kids without putting the whole family into bankruptcy.

Woman: How would *you* know what my sister spends? How would you know what *anybody* spends? You never do any grocery shopping, all *you* do is go out to lunch on your expense account and wave your credit cards around and charge it all to your boss, and then you come home and complain about what *I* spend!

Man: [Very reasonable tone of voice] Why is it, sweetheart, that whenever we try to have a simple adult discussion of any issue, you always get hysterical and turn it into a fight?

Point, set, and match to MAN, you see. Not only doesn't she love him, not only has she fallen for his most obvious move, but he has succeeded in tricking *her* into a posture of violent attack in which she has made a string of open accusations against him that he will be able to remind her of and use again and again in the future. "Darling," he'll be able to say, "the reason I didn't discuss (X) with you before I did it is because you always get so hysterical. Don't you remember the last time I tried to discuss something with you? I made one little remark about our budget, and in thirty seconds you were screaming like a fishwife."

WOMAN does speak English, and she did *hear* that presupposition way back there at the beginning of Confrontation One. Because she heard it and understood it, she knows—as soon as he says, "If you *really* loved me . . ."—that he has done her injury and that she has been wronged. But because she has bungled the confrontation and handed him the victory on a platter, it is WOMAN who will come out of this feeling guilty. We can be 99 percent sure that no matter what goes on in the next few moves, the closing lines will be WOMAN'S apology for her frightful behavior and MAN'S gracious acceptance of that apology.

If a woman goes through enough episodes like this with her husband (or parent or employer or teacher or child or employee or friend or anyone else with whom she must carry on a sustained relationship), a number of unpleasant things will probably happen.

She will grow more and more heavily burdened by guilt with each episode. She feels guilty because she is "always starting fights" with MAN. She feels guilty because she keeps hearing herself—usually to her complete astonishment—shrieking accusations that she knows are childish and semihysterical and frequently unjustified. She feels guilty because she keeps admitting that she does not love this man, which is one of the worst sins she could commit in the Romeo-and-Juliet Wonderland she lives in. The fact that she doesn't know what she is doing—at a conscious level—and that she may love MAN dearly does not help. The guilt is still there. And piled on all this guilt is the guilt she feels because, whether she will admit it or not, she is convinced that somehow she is the one who is being abused here. But no matter how she tries, she cannot put her finger on the source of that conviction. The things MAN says always sound so reasonable, often tender; the things she says always sound vile and stupid. And yet she feels abused and hates herself for that very feeling. This is an unending vicious and multileveled cycle from which she cannot escape.

The relationship may end in separation or divorce. It may end with WOMAN spending an hour a week with a therapist; or even more hours with a doctor, who can never find any explanation for her violent headaches or constant indigestion. It may end with WOMAN becoming a bitter and vindictive harpy, famous for her uncontrollable tongue and temper, and MAN the object of the sympathy of everyone who knows the two of them.

MAN couldn't get away with a continual campaign of *physical* attacks like this. The bruises and marks he would leave would be a testimony to his brutality that would catch up with him in the long run and expose him for the bully that he is. So long as his attacks remain verbal, however, he is not only safe from retribution, he has an excellent chance of being perceived by others as a husband of almost saintly tolerance saddled with a shrewish wife. What is most ironic about this is that he has to do so little to achieve so much. The "If you *really* . . ." move is a baby trick and should not have a prayer of success.

I would like to point out, before the tomatoes come flying, that MAN may not be consciously aware that he is carrying out this constant verbal battery. He may actually believe that he is extraordinarily tolerant and patient and loving, and that his wife is "a mental case."

And we should all be grateful that this is so, because such a man, taught a few elementary facts about verbal behavior and brought to a conscious realization of his actions, will probably change his ways.

He may also be doing it all on purpose, of course,

and enjoying it immensely—and despising WOMAN because she is so pathetic an opponent. The question is, why? And how is he able to do it so easily?

Men, as I said earlier in this book, do get some informal training in the verbal martial arts. They observe other men, and hear or read the speech of other men, and they learn the techniques used by their fathers and their uncles and their older brothers. And they hear utterances like this one:

> "See how your mother acts every time you try to have any kind of discussion with her? Son, I'll never understand women; the better you try to treat them, the less credit you get for it."

In school, where the proportion of male administrators to female teachers is extremely high, young males in America are able to observe one episode after another in which the teacher loses to the administrator's verbal attack—in front of the whole class, in many instances, or at least in front of several males.

By the time they are themselves adult males, men have acquired a body of informal training and information, and a repertoire of challenges and responses, that they have learned so well that they are unaware they ever learned them. Verbal confrontation is as natural to them as walking or breathing, and as unconscious.

Young girls, on the other hand, learn only the techniques of the verbally battered women who are their models, and they move on to produce another generation with exactly the same problems.

There may have been a time when this was not true. The stories of Southern women who ran their families with an iron hand in a tiny rose-colored velvet glove, like the stories of formidable New England matriarchs who kept generations of their kin under control by the mere raising of an eyebrow or the curl of a lip, would lead us to believe that things may once have been different. But in those days women grew up to fill the same roles in society that their mothers and grandmothers had filled before them, or their maiden aunts; and there were generations stretching back into time all secure in the filling of those roles, to pass on an oral tradition. Those days are long gone, however, whether the Equal Rights Amendment is in force or not.

If you look at Confrontation One again, you will see that MAN opens with a challenge in mild Blamer Mode. (If he were more skilled, or had more respect for WOMAN as an opponent, he would use Computer Mode instead; in later chapters we will look at examples of that type.) WOMAN responds immediately to the bait, as he had known she would, in strong Blamer Mode. MAN comes back with an even milder remark than his first one, but WOMAN escalates into violent Blaming. MAN, now the winner and so far out in front that he needn't even exert himself, finishes WOMAN off by ending in a mild combination of Blamer and Computer.

Learn this rule early: NEVER REPLY TO BLAMER MODE WITH ANOTHER BLAMER MODE UTTERANCE. The only way any Blamer ever beats another Blamer is by having more sheer force available—being able to yell louder, knowing more rotten things to say, being able to keep up an exchange of insults longer without running out of steam, or by any similar "advantage." This is exactly analogous to one person beating another in a fight because Person A outweighs Person B by sixty pounds and has a bigger club. It's primitive, and indicates a total lack of skill on both sides.

But if WOMAN should not have replied in Blamer Mode, and should not have taken the bait in (Y), what should she have done? One step at a time . . .

- First Principle: *Know that you are under attack.* Hearing "If you *really* . . ." should have been signal enough.
- Second Principle: *Know what kind of attack you are facing.* Clearly, she wasn't up against much. Any opponent who can't do better for openers than this doesn't have much skill or isn't investing much energy.
- Third Principle: *Know how to make the defense fit the attack.* He gave her an easy one; she should give him an easy one in return. She should speak to the presupposition and do so in Computer Mode. Look at the revised version of Confrontation One, for clarification.

CONFRONTATION ONE—REVISED

Man: If you *really* loved me, you wouldn't waste so much money.

Woman: You know, it's interesting that so many men have this feeling that their wives don't love them.

Notice that she has *not* used "I" or "me." She has *not* taken the bait and moved to defend her spending patterns. She has shown no emotion beyond a kind of neutral interest, and she has not blamed him in any way—she is talking about men *in general.* She also has not admitted that his presupposed claim, that she doesn't love him, is true. Over to MAN.

Carried out in this way, the confrontation may come to a halt right there. For one thing, WOMAN has the advantage of surprise. MAN will be stunned—she is not supposed to know how to carry out a move like that, or to have the fortitude to follow through with it. With any luck at all he'll change the subject as fast as possible, and the whole thing will have been headed off. This is an ideal script and is completely nonviolent self-defense.

To be certain that this is clear, let me show you a violent countermove, for contrast.

CONFRONTATION ONE—REVISED AGAIN

Man: If you *really* loved me, you wouldn't waste so much money.

Woman: You know, it's interesting that so many men—once they reach *your* age—begin to feel that their wives don't love them.

This is dirty fighting. If you give in to the temptation to do this kind of thing, you had better be prepared for an instantaneous escalation, and be sure that you're able to handle some serious heavy-duty confrontation. This is no move for a beginner to make, but many a beginner gets into deep trouble in this way because it is so easy and seems so effective. *Resist the temptation.* File the idea away, so that when an utterance like it is coming *at* you, you will recognize it for the low blow it is. But don't stoop to using it yourself; you can do much better than that, and more honorably.

Now, about the Fourth Principle—following through. If you can't bring yourself to respond as in the first revised Confrontation One because it would spoil MAN's fun, or because you don't have enough self-discipline to ignore the bait about wasting money, you aren't going to do very well at this. You *must* follow through.

Here is a slightly different example:

CONFRONTATION TWO

Child: If you *really* wanted me to get an A in math, you'd buy me a calculator.

Father: A calculator! Do you have any idea how much a calculator *costs?*

Child: Jimmy's dad bought *him* a calculator. So did Mario's.

Father: Jimmy's dad is a *surgeon.* Mario's dad is a very successful *lawyer.* They can *afford* to buy calculators, or any other kind of junk their brats want.

Child: So now I'm a *brat,* and all my friends are brats! Just because you couldn't make it through college like everybody else's dad, just because you're jealous, all of a sudden everybody's a *brat.* That is really *weird,* you know that?

Father: Now, listen, I don't have to take any more of that kind of talk from you!

Child: That's right, you sure don't! Remember that next time you start complaining that I never talk to you about school, okay?

The winner, and the undisputed champeen—CHILD. By FATHER's third move he has completely forgotten that CHILD's math grade was the opener here. He has admitted by default the presupposition that he doesn't really want CHILD to get an A in math. And you can be sure that CHILD will remember this and store it away to use the first time his math grade doesn't meet FATHER's expectations.

Children are often highly skilled in verbal confrontations with their parents, especially in Blamer Mode. Male children hone their skills and increase them as they grow older. Female children are somewhat more likely to accomplish what they want by virtue of their "adorableness," and to rely on their dimples and curls and sitting in people's laps being cute. In the process they forget any verbal skills they might otherwise have acquired; and when they cease to be adorable and are too big to climb into laps anymore, they are utterly vulnerable. If a woman is able to convince a man that she is cute and adorable, it may work. But it is unlikely to work on anyone except a man with whom she is living in an intimate relationship of some kind. Beating your cute little fists against the hairy chest of your boss, your professor, your male colleagues, and so on, WILL NOT WORK. That may be why systems of this kind are ordinarily recommended to women who prefer to remain within the confines of the home; and it shows great good sense on the part of those who devise them that they see this and state it quite frankly in their books, articles, and lectures.

Here's Confrontation Two again, for *you* to revise. You'll find a set of four possible revisions at the end of this chapter, with comments on each. After you've written your own dialogue, you should compare it with those examples—but write yours first.

CONFRONTATION TWO—REVISED

Child: If you *really* wanted me to get an A in math, you'd buy me a calculator.

Father: ______________________________

____

Child: ______________________________

____

Father: ______________________________

____

Child: ______________________________

____

Father: ______________________________

____

Child: ______________________________

____

You may not feel that you need this many moves to finish the confrontation, and that's fine. There are literally an infinite number of possible solutions.

YOUR JOURNAL
SECTION A ATTACKS ON ME:

(1) Date ______________________________

Situation ______________________________

____

FIRST MOVE—What My Opponent Said ____________

____

____

What I Said ______________________________

____

____

What I Should Have Said ______________________________

____

____

SECOND MOVE—What My Opponent Said ____________

____

____

What I Said ______________________________

____

____

What I Should Have Said ______________________________

____

____

THIRD MOVE—What My Opponent Said ____________

____

____

What I Said ____________________________________

____

____

What I Should Have Said ________________________

____

____

FOURTH MOVE—What My Opponent Said __________

____

____

What I Said ____________________________________

____

____

What I Should Have Said ________________________

____

____

(2) Date _______________________________________

Situation ______________________________________

____

FIRST MOVE—What My Opponent Said ____________

____

____

What I Said ______________________________

____

____

What I Should Have Said __________________

____

____

SECOND MOVE—What My Opponent Said ________

____

____

What I Said ______________________________

____

____

What I Should Have Said __________________

____

____

THIRD MOVE—What My Opponent Said _________

____

____

What I Said ______________________________

____

____

What I Should Have Said ____________________

____

____

FOURTH MOVE—What My Opponent Said __________

____

____

What I Said ______________________________

____

____

What I Should Have Said ____________________

____

____

SAMPLE SCRIPTS

CONFRONTATION TWO

Child: If you *really* wanted me to get an A in math, you'd buy me a calculator.

Father: Hey . . . when did you start thinking I didn't care about you getting an A in math?

Child: Well . . . you don't *act* like you care about it. I mean, all the other guys have calculators and stuff, and if they get a good grade on a test, they get a buck for it or something. You never do anything like that. You don't even say I did all right, or anything.

Father: You know, that's pretty stupid of me. Not the calculator part—the reason I don't get you a calculator is because we can't afford it right now—but not paying any attention to your tests or saying anything about them was stupid of me. I'm sorry, and I *do* care about your math grades, and from now on I'll do a better job of letting you know that. Fair enough?

This one is well done, and both CHILD and FATHER come out of it winning. FATHER can afford to bend a little bit, but hasn't obligated himself to buy CHILD a calculator or pay him for his test grades. CHILD is now reassured that FATHER does care about his schoolwork, even if evidence doesn't turn up in the form of money being spent. It's pretty clear that CHILD knows about the money problem and was really only trying to make FATHER understand that *some* attention would be appreciated.

Child: If you *really* wanted me to get an A in math, you'd buy me a calculator.

Father: Parents who *really* want their kids to get A's in math don't buy them calculators. You'll never learn anything about math *that* way. Calculators are just a way of getting out of doing your work.

Child: Then how come you use a calculator when you bring work home from the office?

Father: That is *not* the same thing at all, and you're not so stupid that you can't tell the difference!

FATHER is the loser here and has walked into a sucker punch. Even if he never uses a calculator, the first response to CHILD is all wrong. What FATHER has done here is challenge the wrong presupposition—the trivial one that "a parent who wants a kid to get an A in math always buys that kid a calculator." FATHER may feel that the response is a good one, that he's treating CHILD as a reasonable person who can discuss an issue logically, and that he is offering a challenge to the "you don't really want me to get an A in math" presupposition by presenting an alternative explanation for not buying the calculator. Unfortunately, that's not the way CHILD is going to see or hear it. The message CHILD gets is that he's right—his parent doesn't really care anything about his math grade. Whatever happens from this point on won't change that, and it guarantees a fight. FATHER may "win" in the brute sense, but it will only be because he is bigger, louder, has a better vocabulary, and so on. Very poor strategy, and sure to rebound in the long run.

Child: If you *really* wanted me to get an A in math, you'd buy me a calculator.

Father: If a calculator is what it takes to prove to you that I care about your math grades, son, I'll buy you one.

Child: Can I have one like Fred's got? A really good one?

Father: Like I said, son—if that's what it takes.

This is an interesting variation, and should be examined carefully. FATHER has responded, immediately and directly, to the presupposition in CHILD's opening move. But notice what he has done. First, he's using Placater Mode in response to a child using Blamer Mode, and that's not smart. Children don't feel secure when the people they are trying to look up to as role models and sources of stability in their world start Placating them. CHILD is dissatisfied enough to push it further; his second move is a compressed "If you *really* mean it when you say you want me to get an A in math, you won't just buy me *any* old calculator, you'll get me a fancy, expensive one like Fred's." And FATHER does it again—more Placating.

And that's not all. If you take a close look at what

FATHER is saying, you'll notice a new presupposition that's being sneaked in, something like this:

> "You are the kind of kid that can only be convinced about my wanting you to get an A if I *buy* you something, and I don't think much of that kind of kid—but I guess I'm stuck with you."

It's a small dig, going by fast, but it's in there, and CHILD will hear it. Especially when FATHER repeats it for him. Nobody won here, and nobody got anything he wanted. This is a standoff in every way, with the possible exception of FATHER's finances.

Child: If you *really* wanted me to get an A in math, you'd buy me a calculator.

Father: Why do you think I don't want you to get an A in math, son? That's a crazy idea.

Child: I didn't say that! *You* said that! You're always putting stuff in my mouth I don't say!

Father: Now, getting all excited and starting an argument is not going to help your math or anything else. When you're ready to talk like a reasonable person, we'll discuss this again.

FATHER's mistake here was in adding "That's a crazy idea" to the end of his first response. Up to that point, the response was a neutral request for information about the presupposition. But the "crazy idea" addition is straight Blamer Mode, and it shames and embarrasses the child. In the sense that FATHER doesn't have to buy a calculator and has demonstrated his superior status in the household relative to CHILD, FATHER has won. But the price is a resentful and humiliated CHILD who still believes that FATHER doesn't care anything about his math grades and may now be convinced that the reason for that is that he doesn't have any respect for CHILD in any case. Resist the temptation to throw in little flourishes and extras, unless you have had time to plan them carefully and are very sure what presuppositions they carry with them.

Section B Attacks

If You *Really* . . . (II)

5

Going from Section A moves to Section B moves will not be difficult, because Section B is only Section A with the power turned up one notch. Your practice with the examples in Chapter Four should make it possible for you to move through this chapter with ease and confidence. Keep the Four Principles in mind; keep the Satir Modes in mind; and *practice.*

The surface structure for a Section B move looks like this:

If you *really* (X), you would/wouldn't *want* to (Y).

Or, to make it just a tad meaner . . .

"If you *really* (X), you wouldn't even *want* to (Y)."
(Or) . . . you would at least *want* to (Y)."

There are two presuppositions in the basic sequence that you need to pay attention to. The first one is already familiar: "You don't really (X)." And then there is this one:

"You have the power to control not just your actions but also your personal desires."

The first presupposition may or may not be false, depend-

Your Personal Octagon

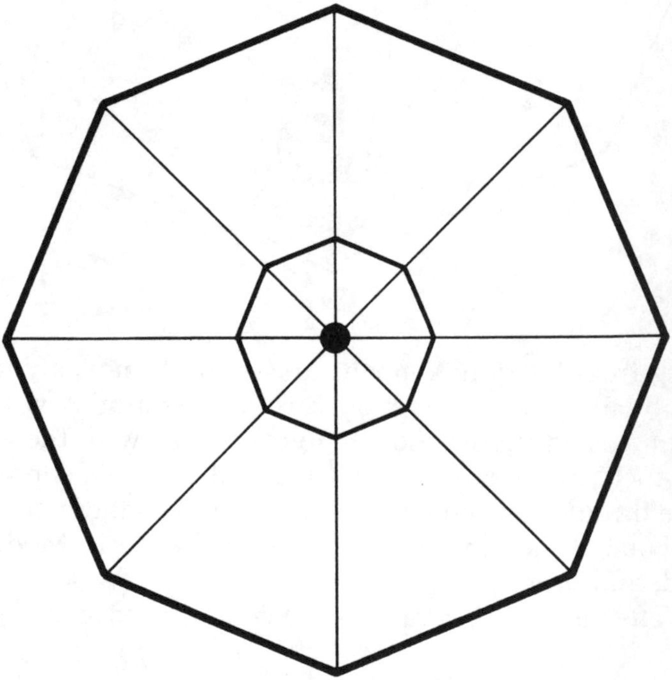

ing on whether you really do or do not love someone, want to get good grades, want to be promoted, want to make your mother proud of you, want to make the football team, want to stop smoking, or whatever is the content of (X). The second presupposition, however, is *always false.*

All of us are able to exercise our willpower to a certain extent. We may be quite capable of turning down that second piece of cake. We may be equally capable of staying out of that poker game we were invited to join. But none of us, because we are human and because desire is part of being human, is able to deliberately NOT WANT the piece of cake or NOT WANT to join the game. We may be able to distract ourselves by eating four carrots instead of the cake or by going fishing instead of to the poker game, thus lowering the intensity of the desire a little—but the wanting remains. That is the nature of being human, and if you are free of that trait, you certainly don't need to read this book.

In a Section B confrontation you will have no trouble recognizing the attack. There's "if you *really*" to let you know something's up, and once you've spotted the two presuppositions you know what you're dealing with. The level of skill and strength shown is slightly higher than a Section A move, but it's nothing formidable. You know that the proper way to handle it is to respond to the presupposition, preferably with no violence at all. But there's an additional problem here: *which* presupposition? The Section B move offers you two.

The answer is that it depends. Which one is the strongest attack on you? Which one bothers you most? Which one seems the easier to take on? You have ample time to move against both if you like, and it makes no particular difference which one you start with. This is nothing to be distracted about; choose one, and then go on to the other if it turns out to be necessary.

Here's an example for you:

CONFRONTATION THREE

Mother: If you *really* cared anything about my health, you wouldn't *want* to dress the way you do!

Daughter: There is nothing wrong with the way I dress except that you are too old to understand what a young woman *ought* to wear!

Mother: What? I'm not old, and if I wasn't so sick, I wouldn't look old, either. How can you *be* so cruel? My own daughter! But never mind—you know me, I don't care about anything anymore.

Daughter: Mother, I didn't mean that you look old, I didn't mean *any* of that like it sounded. Mother, don't cry, *please* don't cry! You know how I am, I say things before I think; I never did have any sense. You know I wouldn't hurt you for anything in the world.

Mother: No, it's my fault, and you're right. I'm an old woman, and I'm holding you back. But I won't be here much longer, and then you can wear whatever you want to wear.

Daughter: Oh, heavens, Mother, you know I don't care what I wear! Come on, now—what do you hate the most? You tell me, and I'll throw it away. Please?

Notice the sequence of moves here. MOTHER opens as mild Blamer. DAUGHTER falls for the bait; she ignores the presuppositions and concedes both that she doesn't care about her mother's health and that she is able to control her desires—thereby implicitly admitting that she deliberately mistreats her mother. Since she has admitted that she could stop *wanting* to dress the way she does if she cared to, no other conclusion is possible. With both her admissions made, DAUGHTER responds in strong Blamer Mode. MOTHER grabs her opportunity and surges into Distracter Mode, raining blows in all directions, and—sure enough—DAUGHTER instantly switches to Placater. MOTHER does a touch of phony Placating, and then twists the knife in for a final Blamer claim; DAUGHTER, she accuses, is just hanging around waiting for her to die so that she can dress like a fool and spend the rest of her life in that stupid activity. DAUGHTER, now completely demoralized, goes into the most extreme Placater style she can muster, and ends by begging for a chance to prove that she is not really the monster she has just admitted herself to be.

Because I have no intention of writing a sexist book, I was very careful to include in Confrontation Three a *woman* who is highly skilled at verbal abuse. While it's true that men are more likely to be good at this than women, by no means are all women innocent victims. MOTHER in this example is guilty of blatant child abuse, but like the man in Confrontation One, her attacks leave no surface bruises. If she is good at what she does, she may manage to live out her life viewed by one and all as a devoted parent mistreated and neglected by her ungrateful selfish child. Because she's a woman and must deal with the stereotype of the endlessly complaining older woman, it's a little harder for her to bring it off. But if she does it with dignity and elegance (yes, this is possible), and if the child makes one stupid mistake after another, her chances are pretty good.

Now, let's consider what DAUGHTER might have done instead. A few possibilities . . .

CONFRONTATION THREE—REVISED

Mother: If you *really* cared anything about my health, you wouldn't *want* to dress the way you do!

Daughter: The idea that people don't care about other people's health is interesting, don't you think? It would seem that any human being would, just naturally, be concerned about the well-being of other people . . . but just look at the state of health care in this country!

This is a response in full Computer Mode, directed to the first presupposition. MOTHER and DAUGHTER are now in the midst of a philosophical discussion of an abstract question instead of a personal confrontation. Or . . .

Mother: If you *really* cared anything about my health, you wouldn't *want* to dress the way you do!

Daughter: You know, the idea that people are able to control not only their actions but their desires is a fascinating one.

This is the same technique, but DAUGHTER has responded to the second presupposition rather than the first.

Or DAUGHTER might want to try something in a phony Leveler Mode. For the beginner, this is most easily done with a "when" question, an absolutely straight face, and an air of neutral interest, like this:

Daughter: Mother, when did you start thinking that I don't care anything about your health?

OR . . .

Daughter: Mother, have you always thought that people could control their wishes and their desires?

The phony Leveler stance is a useful one, but it must be done with care. Any mistake in the tone of voice or the expression of the face, and the utterance will sound like Blaming instead of Leveling. Above all, be sure you don't throw any "evens" into one of these, as in this example:

Daughter: Mother, when did you first decide that I don't even care about your health?

The other question words (WH-words) are also available for use in this move. For instance:

- "Where did you get the idea that I don't care about your health?"
- "Why do you suppose you feel that I don't care anything about your health?"
- "Who in the world suggested to you that I didn't care anything about your health?"
(and so on . . .)

But be careful with these; each carries with it a presupposition. The first: You got the idea that I don't care about your health *somewhere*. The second: You have some reason for feeling that I don't care about your health, if we could only figure out what it is. The third: Someone suggested to you that I didn't care anything about your health.

Any question about time will also have presuppositions, but a time question is not as tricky to handle and not as likely to lead you into dropping in a presupposition that you never intended. The "when" question usually leaves your opponent only two choices: either answer the question as if it were really a neutral request for information or deny its presupposition. Like this:

Daughter: Mother, when did you first start thinking that I don't care anything about your health?

Mother: When you were thirteen years old, that's when. Don't you remember the time that . . .
[And with any luck at all, MOTHER will head off into an anecdote, and you'll be able to shift to another subject entirely.]

OR . . .

Mother: I never said I thought you didn't care about my health! *I* was talking about the disgusting way you *dress!*

Now MOTHER should move into a lengthy lecture on proper clothing; but whatever happens, she has been forced to switch her techniques and *she* is now on the defensive. If things become too difficult, this one can be tied off with a phony Placater stance, as in this example:

Daughter: Isn't it amazing how I always misunderstand you, dear? I must not be paying attention, or else I'm just stupid. I'll try to do better.

DAUGHTER has really won with this last line, although it may sound like a surrender. She has not admitted either that she can control her wishes or that she doesn't care about MOTHER's health; she took care of that with her original "when" question. She has led the confrontation completely away from either MOTHER's health or her own style of dress and has not agreed to change that style in any way whatsoever. Finally, she has demonstrated what a good DAUGHTER she is by admitting a trivial flaw—not paying close enough attention when spoken to—and promising to improve her performance in the future. MOTHER may not be taken in by any of this; but for her to work her way back to either of the two attacks she started with will require *her* to behave like a shrew, become violent and semihysterical, and that is not the way to win.

If you have no choice but to hit back, the counterattack to the opening line in Confrontation Three goes like this:

Daughter: When a woman reaches your age, dear, she often begins to think that nobody cares about

> her health. It's very common, and perfectly understandable, and you mustn't worry about it for a single minute.

This is something you reserve for emergencies. As in any other martial art, unnecessary force is dishonorable and merely indicates that you are either an amateur or a sadist. It may be justified as a way of protecting someone else who is clearly at the mercy of a vindictive parent, one who would stoop to attacking his or her own child in public. Don't be surprised, however, if your attempt to help out in a situation like that causes the child to turn on you and defend the rotten parent! That's a pretty standard script, especially if the child is one of those completely unaware victims and the attacks have been going on for years. Attacking *you* may be the only chance the victim gets to ease the burden of guilt—if it happens, *let it pass.* You can afford to be generous, and she probably cannot.

Now, here is a sample confrontation for you to work on, with suggested solutions at the end of the chapter:

CONFRONTATION FOUR

Supervisor: If you *really* cared about being promoted, you'd *want* to get your reports in on time, like everybody else in the department does.

Employee: ____________________

____

____

Supervisor: ____________________

____

____

Employee: ______________________________________

____

____

(Who won?)

YOUR JOURNAL
SECTION B ATTACKS ON ME:

(1) Date ____________________

Situation ____________________

____

FIRST MOVE—What My Opponent Said ____________________

____

____

What I Said ____________________

____

____

What I Should Have Said ____________________

____

____

SECOND MOVE—What My Opponent Said ____________________

____

____

What I Said ____________________

____

____

What I Should Have Said ____________________

____

____

THIRD MOVE—What My Opponent Said ___________

____

____

What I Said _______________________________

____

____

What I Should Have Said ___________________

____

____

FOURTH MOVE—What My Opponent Said _________

____

____

What I Said _______________________________

____

____

What I Should Have Said ___________________

____

____

(2) Date ___________________________________

Situation _________________________________

____

FIRST MOVE—What My Opponent Said ___________

____

____

What I Said ______________________________

____

____

What I Should Have Said ____________________

____

____

SECOND MOVE—What My Opponent Said ________

____

____

What I Said ______________________________

____

____

What I Should Have Said ____________________

____

____

THIRD MOVE—What My Opponent Said __________

____

____

What I Said ______________________________

____

____

What I Should Have Said ______________________

____

____

FOURTH MOVE—What My Opponent Said __________

____

____

What I Said __________________________________

____

____

What I Should Have Said ______________________

____

____

SAMPLE SCRIPTS

CONFRONTATION FOUR

Supervisor: If you *really* cared about being promoted, you'd *want* to get your reports in on time, like everybody else in the department does.

Employee: Miss Stein, have you always felt that I had no interest in being promoted?

Supervisor: No—frankly, my first reaction to you was that you were someone with a lot of ambition. I expected you to get ahead in the department and do it pretty quickly.

Employee: I wonder what caused you to question your original judgment, Miss Stein. Ordinarily you trust your perceptions of your staff, and that policy seems to have had only positive results for the firm.

EMPLOYEE has done this well. Miss Stein is now in a tight position for her next move. She may of course move right in with a response like this:

"Thank you; I appreciate the compliment. However, in *your* case I clearly was mistaken."

If that happens, however, EMPLOYEE has nevertheless managed one important and positive result—Miss Stein has switched into Leveler Mode, and it should now be possible to discuss the issue more openly and reasonably. EMPLOYEE has not made the mistake of taking the bait and arguing about the timing of the reports, but has responded to the presupposition. Furthermore, although a compliment has been paid to the SUPERVISOR, it isn't an excessive Placating gush. It is moderate, and primarily in Computer Mode. Miss Stein may be willing to accept it and unwilling to present the idea that she has been mistaken in her perceptions this time. In either case, EMPLOYEE is now in a much better position to discuss the matter.

Supervisor: If you *really* cared about being promoted, you'd *want* to get your reports in on time, like everybody else in the department does.

Employee: Miss Stein, where did you get the idea that I'm not interested in being promoted?

Supervisor: [*Icily*] If you are suggesting that I have listened to gossip about you, or anything of that nature, I suggest you think carefully before you say anything more. I *despise* office gossip.

Employee: Oh, I didn't mean to suggest *anything* like *that*, Miss Stein!

[To which, I'm afraid, the most likely response is "Then why *did* you suggest it?"]

EMPLOYEE has properly moved to respond to the presupposition in this confrontation. However, what happened is typical of the hazards of asking anything but a time question. Each of the WH-question words (who, what, when, where, how, why, and so on) has presuppositions of its own. Since the person using a Section B has already agreed to the existence of the claim being made after "If you *really* . . ." that existence has to have had a starting point in time. Asking about that point is then no challenge. This strategy may be boring, but your goal is not excitement, even the excitement of verbal violence. Your goal is to avoid that violence as far as possible, to do so honorably, and (when it cannot be avoided) to handle it in such a way that you cease to be its victim without yourself becoming an attacker. Stay with the "when" questions until you are certain you are ready to move beyond them or that it is truly necessary to do so.

Supervisor: If you *really* cared about being promoted, you'd *want* to get your reports in on time, like everybody else in the department does.

Employee: Miss Stein, do you really believe that people have the ability to control their desires as well as their actions?

Supervisor: I beg your pardon?

Employee: I mean, when did you start thinking that people had control over what they *want* to do?

EMPLOYEE has slipped badly here and has chosen the wrong presupposition to respond to. Miss Stein is understandably bewildered by the whole exchange, and things are only going to get worse. You would only take up the question of whether someone can control their desires when the issue being discussed is food or drink or sex or gambling or something of equal importance. The idea of anyone agonizing over whether they do or do not want to get their reports in on time, fighting or resisting the temptation to get them in late or early, is preposterous. And EMPLOYEE can only come out of this looking ridiculous. SUPERVISOR wins again.

Supervisor: If you *really* cared about being promoted, you'd *want* to get your reports in on time, like everybody else in the department does.

Employee: Miss Stein, when did you begin to feel that I am not interested in promotion?

Supervisor: I should think that would be obvious—when you began turning in your reports late.

Employee: Perhaps a specific incident would be helpful, Miss Stein.

You can always hope that this won't happen. And whether it happens or not has much to do with whether Miss Stein is in fact justified in complaining about the lateness of your reports or not, as well as whether that lateness is something unique to you and not shared by your fellow workers. However, if you are not going to be able to avoid dealing with the accusation, you are far better off discussing a particular occasion on which it is claimed that you were at fault. You may be able to explain that instance to your supervisor's satisfaction and convince her that it isn't part of a pattern, but an isolated event. If you are actually at fault, and have no excuse, and if it *is* part of a general pattern, the fact that you are able to discuss it reasonably may win you a little time to improve your performance. If Miss Stein cannot come up with a specific incident and is forced to admit that, you have gained a point or two. It's much too early in this one to see who will win, but given the SUPERVISOR's second move, it is going along properly. EMPLOYEE should stay in Computer Mode, unless it becomes possible to move to genuine Leveling, and should try to carry this off with as much dignity as the facts of the matter will allow.

One word of warning: Probably the stupidest move of all, the most nonproductive that you could make, would be to go for the last succulent morsel of the bait and maneuver yourself into an argument about whether other employees get their reports in on time. Don't stoop to that. Even if you know for a fact that half the staff is always later than you are, saying so will only make it possible for your supervisor to call you a tattletale. Tattletales are not admired in this country, even when they are in the right. Let that pass, even if SUPERVISOR makes an all-out effort to force you to get into it. If you find yourself obliged to say, "Miss Stein, I do not talk about other people behind their backs," you may feel that you're risking insolence and asking for trouble. On the contrary—you will be respected for it. Your failure to take that position will earn you nothing but contempt, whether it shows in the surface responses made to you or not.

Section C Attacks

Don't You Even *Care*. . .

6

This technique is a major advance over those in Sections A and B. It's basic form is like this:

Don't you even *care* about (X)?

Possible fillers for (X) are infinite in number; here are some typical examples.

Don't you even *care* about . . .

- your grades?
- your children?

- your colleagues?
- your students?
- your patients?
- your appearance?
- your health?
- your responsibility to (Y)?

In skilled hands the range is awe-inspiring, with items such as "Don't you even *care* about the countless generations to come who will have to pay the price for your misguided actions?" representing a middle level of potency.

The presuppositions that have to be identified for Section C moves are these:

- "You don't care about (X)."
- "You *should* care about (X); you're rotten not to.
- "Therefore, you should feel very guilty about this."

As you would suspect, the presence of the word "even" hammers in the third presupposition. If Section C challenges are used without "even," they are considerably more gentle. Coming from a Leveler they may be no more than a genuinely neutral request for information about your feelings. When you hear a Section C with "even" in it, however, you may be reasonably confident that the question isn't neutral and that a confrontation is headed your way.

You'll notice a specific difference between this move and the Section B move. Both have more than one presupposition for you to deal with. But in "If you *really* (X), you would/wouldn't *want* to (Y)" there doesn't have to be any relationship between (X) and (Y). They are completely independent of each other, and almost anything to which the victim is vulnerable can be used to fill the (Y) slot.

This isn't true with a Section C move; here the second and third presuppositions depend upon the first. Obviously, if your opponent is wrong and you *do* care about (X), then the second and third presuppositions are irrelevant.

There are a number of possible ways to handle a Section C. A crude one, but an effective move if you don't mind following through on it, is this:

Chair: Don't you even *care* about the other members of this committee?

Member: No; why?

Your Personal Octagon

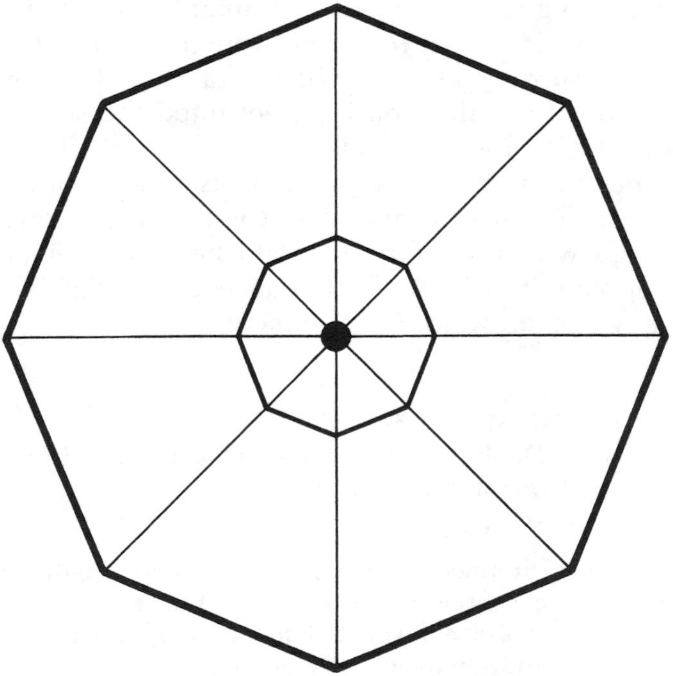

I'm serious. There are times when a crude move—like a two-by-four right between the eyes—can be most effective. The biggest advantage of this response is its shock value.

Look again at the presuppositions of a Section C, and it will be clear why the outrageous "No; why?" is an effective response. The person coming at you with a Section C is relying on you to go along with the idea that *nobody* with even a shred of human decency could possibly disagree with those presuppositions. Nobody. Your opponent expects you to agree that the item in (X) is something everyone approves of, that not to go along with that is wicked and rotten and abominable in every way, and that anyone guilty of the accusation should feel like a worm and beg to be stepped on. Your anticipated response is a furious claim that *of course* you care about (X), and how *dare* your opponent suggest that you don't—which means, of course, that you have accepted the second and third presuppositions by default.

Unless you have a reputation as a sociopath or an eccentric, the possibility that you will not go along with this script will never for an instant have been imagined. Your opponent will be flabbergasted, and that may be exactly what you want. For instance:

CONFRONTATION FIVE

Teacher: Don't you even *care* about your little girl flunking out of third grade?

Parent: No; why?

Teacher: [Stunned silence of considerable length] But you can't possibly mean that! You're a good parent, you're a respected member of the community, and you *love* your daughter!

Parent: [Maintains neutral expression of polite interest, but says nothing at all.]

Teacher: Look, let me explain to you what it means for a child to flunk a grade and get kept back. *First* of all . . .

PARENT has won hands down. TEACHER has completely forgotten (or will have by the time he or she is a sentence or two farther along) that the opener was essentially an attack on the parent's moral fitness to *be* a parent. What TEACHER will do now is present a lengthy lecture on the problems of a flunking child—any flunking child at all, not the one who is associated with PARENT. The confrontation has been successfully defused from a personal attack to a philosophical discussion. PARENT, if skillful, will agree with everything TEACHER says that is remotely sensible and at the first opportunity will increase the degree of distance between the personal and the philosophical. For example:

Parent: You know, you're absolutely right, and it takes someone with your training and experience to realize the implications of these matters. And as long as you've brought it up, don't you think that everything you're saying also applies to college students? Sure, they're adults, but even so, it seems to me—

Teacher: Certainly! Many people do not realize the burden that an F in just one course places on a hard-working student. When I took Logic, for example—now please remember that I was a straight-A student in every other class I had in college—but when I took *Logic* . . .

Only after PARENT is long gone will TEACHER realize that he or she has been had, since obviously no person who really did not care about his own child flunking third grade would have spent an hour discussing the dreadful consequences of flunking.

What happens next in the continuing relationship between PARENT and TEACHER (not to mention the one between PARENT and FLUNKING CHILD!) depends upon the real-world situation. But the technique itself should be clear to you. However, it has one flaw that must be pointed out immediately: You can never use it twice with the same opponent. If you try it a second time, you're going to hear an icy "You surely don't think you can put that over on me *again,* do you?" Precisely because it is such a stunner, and precisely because it is so crude, it will be remembered. Its effectiveness is probably limited even in the sense that you can only use it with one member of a given group in the circle of people you deal with. You are otherwise likely to hear this: "You surely don't think you can get past *me* with that just because you managed to put it over on TEACHER, do you?" But it has its place, and when you are in that place, by all means put it to use.

Another possibility, and one with a bit wider application, is to respond immediately to the first presupposition, but not by denying it. Instead, present a question about the presupposition. For example:

Employer: Don't you even *care* about the way sales have been dropping off in your division?

Employee: Pardon me, Mr. Lopez, but when did you first start thinking I had no interest in our sales figures?

OR . . .

Employee: Do you see this indifference to the sales figures as a general problem, Mr. Lopez, or do you feel that it's confined to the division chiefs in the PQR Plant?

OR . . .

Employee: That question is certainly worth exploring; however, before any attempt can be made to answer it, there is the problem of actually putting one's finger on the *cause* for this indifference to sales that you've noticed. A number of factors that might account for it come to mind, but your perception of the matter—from where you sit—would constitute a valuable source of preliminary data.

If we gave belts in verbal self-defense, each of the three replies above would represent a more highly valued belt color. And it can certainly be carried much farther. In business or professional contexts, one of your surest responses to a Section C is a question *about* the first presupposition (that you "don't even *care*") as heavily larded with the jargon of your field as you can make it. If you can do this entirely in Computer Mode, with no hint of "I" or emotion anywhere, you have an excellent chance of leaving your opponent exhausted in three moves.

And while we are on the subject of the world of business and the professions, I'd like to focus briefly on one of the factors that gives men an advantage over women in this part of the arena. An amazingly high percentage of men, with absolute honesty, are astonished when they find that the verbal attacks they've carried out in the courtroom or at the conference table are resented by a woman on the receiving end. THEY ARE NOT PRETENDING; THEY TRULY DO NOT UNDERSTAND.

Males learn very early that verbal confrontations are a part of the necessary activity of their careers. They learn to admire the skilled verbal infighter, to keep track of the "one for you, and one for me" scores as the confrontations go along, and they do not take any of this personally. (The man who doesn't learn this is the man who gets passed over again and again while less able people are promoted over his head.)

Women are bewildered when they see two men who have just spent twenty minutes trading the sort of vicious insults associated with lifelong hatred go off to lunch together as if nothing at all had happened. Men are equally bewildered when they find that the woman they just went through the same process with won't go to lunch because she's angry. They see it as roughly equivalent to refusing to go to lunch with someone because you were just whipped at checkers. And when their "But you weren't supposed to take any of that personally, don't you know that?" is either not believed or considered to be insult piled upon injury, they are reinforced in their belief that women have no business in business.

The fact that women are frequently unable to play this game—and make no mistake about it, it is just that, a game—limits them forever to the lower strata of most corporations, universities, hospitals, publishing houses, and so on. Men look upon it much as they do any other sport: Get in there and play to win, and then, after the final whistle blows, everybody go out together for pizza and beer. (Or steak and a good red wine, or doughnuts and coffee, depending.)

If you are a woman and you do not own the corporation, publishing firm, hospital, or whatever—which would change all the rules in a number of intricate ways—either learn to play the game or forget about a career within the system. I'm sure this statement is not going to be looked upon with any pleasure by people of either sex; but it is the grim truth, and nothing will be gained by pretending that it isn't. If you go into a football game and insist upon playing it by the rules of tennis, you surely have better sense than to think that (a) you will win; or (b) anybody will ever let you play in their football game again.

Two more rules, especially for women: Do not cry.

Not EVER. No matter what. A man might under extraordinary circumstances be able to get away with it, but a woman can't. And don't ever forget for one moment that the rules of the game apply just as rigidly to the other women present as they do to the men.

The second rule is included because I have seen so many women who handled the confrontation game with casual ease in the usual team situation of one woman and seventeen men, but were completely disoriented when another woman joined the group. Please remember that the other woman is not attacking you personally any more than the men are. Like you, she is simply playing the game as well as she can.

I have heard men say, with utter seriousness, "But it wasn't a lie at *all*—not in *that* situation." Whether it was true or not, they will explain solemnly, has nothing to do with whether it was a lie. Women must learn to anticipate this orientation toward honesty and to take it into account in planning verbal strategy.

(Later in this book you will find special chapters for men and for women, where male-female differences in verbal behavior will be discussed in more detail.)

When the totally abstract Section C move comes at you, in business or in any other setting, your response should take advantage of that abstractness. For example:

> *Opponent:* Don't you even *care* about the thousands of people who go to bed hungry in this country every night?

This is a *low* thing to say. Of course you care. The idea that you don't, that perhaps you sit at night stuffing your face with chocolates and chuckling over the image of tiny children crying with swollen bellies in the slums, giggling over the elderly couple splitting a can of cat food for dinner . . . that is repulsive. For somebody to accuse you of that is not to be looked upon as just a passing remark. It's arsenic in your potato salad, and unless it's true it's inexcusable. The very last thing you should do is stoop to quibbling over how much you care. (A little bit. A whole lot. A rating of 3.2 on a scale from 1 to 5.) DO NOT FALL FOR THIS. Instead, you say back

> "Which study are you referring to on that, Dana? The Calumet Institute Report or the one from the Borogrovian Center for Social Research?"

And make them both up. And stoutly maintain, in the face of all inquiries, that you are *shocked* to hear that your opponent has not even read (the "even" is important!) either of these two major studies. After all, you must point out, if he or she *really* cared about hungry people, he would at least take the trouble to keep up with the basic literature on the subject!

Now, here are two practice sets for you to work on. Sample scripts are at the end of the chapter.

CONFRONTATION SIX

Doctor: Don't you even *care* about the effect your smoking has on the health of your husband and children?

Patient: ____

____

____

Doctor: ____

____

____

Patient: ____

(Who won?)

CONFRONTATION SEVEN

Mother: Don't you even *care* what your father will say when he hears that you're dropping out of school? Don't you even *care* about the way that will make him feel?

Student:

Mother:

Student:

(Who won?)

YOUR JOURNAL
SECTION C ATTACKS ON ME:

(1) Date ______________________________

Situation ______________________________

____

FIRST MOVE—What My Opponent Said ______________________________

____

____

What I Said ______________________________

____

____

What I Should Have Said ______________________________

____

____

SECOND MOVE—What My Opponent Said ______________________________

____

____

What I Said ______________________________

____

____

What I Should Have Said ______________________________

____

____

THIRD MOVE—What My Opponent Said ____________

____

____

What I Said ________________________________

____

____

What I Should Have Said ______________________

____

____

FOURTH MOVE—What My Opponent Said __________

____

____

What I Said ________________________________

____

____

What I Should Have Said ______________________

____

____

(2) Date ___________________________________

Situation __________________________________

____

FIRST MOVE—What My Opponent Said ____________

What I Said

What I Should Have Said

SECOND MOVE—What My Opponent Said

What I Said

What I Should Have Said

THIRD MOVE—What My Opponent Said

What I Said

What I Should Have Said ____________________

____

____

FOURTH MOVE—What My Opponent Said __________

____

____

What I Said ________________________________

____

____

What I Should Have Said ____________________

____

____

SAMPLE SCRIPTS

CONFRONTATION SIX

Doctor: Don't you even *care* about the effect your smoking has on the health of your husband and children?

Patient: Well, *he* smokes, too. Why don't you talk to *him* about smoking?

Doctor: Because he isn't my patient. *You* are my patient.

Patient: Well, it's not fair.

PATIENT here has swallowed the bait, admitted by default that she doesn't care at all what her smoking does to her family's health (which is very unlikely to be true), and has done her best to dump part of the blame on one of the people she is accused of endangering. There *are* worse ways of handling this, but not many.

Doctor: Don't you even *care* about the effect your smoking has on the health of your husband and children?

Patient: Yes, of course I care. You know perfectly well that I care. And I resent *very* much your attempt to make me feel even worse about it than I feel already.

Doctor: Then why in the world do you keep on smoking?

Patient: Because, as you are also perfectly well aware, I am addicted to cigarettes.

PATIENT is winning, but not by the usual techniques. The verbal confrontation between doctor and patient—and especially between male doctor and female patient—is one of the two or three trickiest interactions in the world of communication. PATIENT should be safe in Leveling with the DOCTOR—that is why she goes to him, presumably, to tell him the truth and pay him for using his expertise to help her with whatever problems that truth may involve. PATIENT has tackled this situation head-on and informed DOCTOR that she will not tolerate his attempt to increase the guilt she already feels by asking her questions to which he already knows the answers. She is announcing, "I will not play that game." Remember that there probably exists no situation between any doctor and patient in which the doctor does not hold the dominant position. The usual rules don't hold, as a result, and you must be exceedingly careful.

Doctor: Don't you even *care* about the effect your smoking has on the health of your husband and children?

Patient: No. Why?

Doctor: Hmmmmm. [Makes a note in PATIENT's file.]

Patient: Well?

PATIENT is not only losing but is in big trouble.

DOCTOR, because of his or her unique status in American society, is not the proper person to try this on. Nor is any doctor someone on whom to try dropping the names of phony research on the dangers of smoking. DOCTOR, if worth the money you're spending, has read all the studies and knows the facts. PATIENT is going to end up in very deep water with such maneuvers. In this example, the note to PATIENT's file is likely to say something like this: "Patient states that she is indifferent to the harm her smoking may cause her family." And it will be followed by what DOCTOR thinks that indicates in terms of PATIENT's physical or emotional health. PATIENT has goofed.

Doctor: Don't you even *care* about the effect your smoking has on the health of your husband and children?

Patient: You've been my doctor for six years now, if my memory serves me right. When did you first start thinking that I was indifferent to my family's health?

Doctor: After the fiftieth time I told you you had to quit smoking, explained to you that you were endangering not only your own health but that of everyone in your family, and saw you go right on smoking.

Patient: A doctor ought to know better than that. Does your experience and research lead you to believe that it's possible to cure addictions by the use of logical arguments? If so, the news has not yet trickled down to the general public.

This is very well done, and PATIENT is—probably—winning. There is always the outside possibility that DOCTOR will be so outraged at PATIENT's attempt to even up the dominance relations between them slightly that he or she will make a little note like this one: "Patient appears belligerent when challenged on her refusal to comply with medical orders to stop smoking." But she is doing the best that can be done under the circumstances.

CONFRONTATION SEVEN

Mother: Don't you even *care* what your father will say when he hears that you're dropping out of school? Don't you even *care* about the way that will make him feel?

Student: No. Do you think I should care?

Mother: What kind of a monster *are* you, anyway? As hard as your father has worked to pay for your education, the things he's done without—how can you sit there and face me and say that you don't care?

Student: Because, Mother, it happens to be the truth. I'm not all that proud of it, but it's the truth. It was Dad's idea for me to go to college, not mine, and it was a rotten idea to begin with. The sooner we put it out of its misery, the better off everybody—including Dad—will be.

This is properly done, although STUDENT may feel miserable doing it. MOTHER here is doing a classic Blaming attack and, if allowed to continue, will soon bring in Dad's heart condition and the time he walked five miles through a blizzard to buy STUDENT something or other for Christmas, and far on into the night. It has to be made clear to her, as gently as possible, that this won't work. If STUDENT is telling the truth and the whole college scheme was Dad's idea and is never going to go anywhere but downhill, then it should be brought to an end. It may make Dad feel awful, but not as awful as he will feel if it goes on. College is not what everyone wants or needs, nor should it be; and if it is all wrong for this student, no favors are being done to anyone by continuing to throw good money (and energy) after bad. STUDENT is winning.

Mother: Don't you even *care* what your father will say when he hears that you're dropping out of school? Don't you even *care* about the way that will make him feel?

Student: When did you start thinking I didn't care anything about Dad's feelings, Mother?

Mother: When you stopped even pretending to do your schoolwork and started spending all your time lying around at parties and acting the way you do.

Student: Then why don't we talk about *that?* It's obviously what's really bothering you.

It's hard to know exactly where this will go—at the moment we have a standoff. STUDENT has, quite properly, questioned the presupposition instead of taking the bait. MOTHER has responded with even more Blaming and has accused STUDENT of several unpleasant things. STUDENT would have been better off resisting the temptation to add "It's obviously what's really bothering you" to the end of the next move, in my opinion. This is likely to provoke "Oh, you always think you know everything!" and turn into a brawl instead of the reasonable discussion that is needed.

Mother: Don't you even *care* what your father will say when he hears that you're dropping out of school? Don't you even *care* about the way that will make him feel?

Student: That's a pretty common idea . . . that someone who drops out of school after their parents made a lot of sacrifices just for that purpose isn't even *bothered* about it. But I never expected to hear it from you, Mother.

Mother: Oh? Why not?

Student: Because you're not the kind of person who would make that kind of stereotyped judgment, that's why not.

Very well done. MOTHER has been complimented thoroughly, the presupposition has been challenged, the STUDENT is in a mild Computer Mode, and all is going as it should. The next move is up to MOTHER, who is going to have to change strategies or look more foolish than she probably cares to.

Mother: Don't you even *care* what your father will say when he hears that you're dropping out of school? Don't you even *care* about the way that will make him feel?

Student: Now you're going to start laying all those guilt trips on me, aren't you?

Mother: I beg your pardon?

Student: First you're going to tell me how hard you and Dad worked to get me into college. Then you're going to tell me that you never took a vacation, not even once, so there'd be enough money to pay my tuition. Right? Then you're going to start on Dad's heart condition, and how that's all my fault, and then, Mother darling, to finish it off, you're going to tell me that if I drop out of school, it will kill him, and I'll have that on my conscience for the rest of my life. *Aren't* you?

Now MOTHER is going to tell STUDENT, with quantities of ice, that he or she is contemptible. She has won, and so long as STUDENT insists on this technique, she will always win. This is a sad way to spend your life—please don't do it. At the time it feels wonderful, especially if you have heard MOTHER run through that particular speech hundreds of times already. But the end results are not worth the two or three minutes of gratification. You are only reinforcing MOTHER in this pattern of verbal attack by showing that it will work so well on you.

Section D Attacks

Even *You* Should . . .

7

The most basic form of the Section D attack is not very subtle and certainly should be hard to overlook. The very first word is "Even," and the strong stress on whatever follows makes the fact that this is an attack unmistakable. Notice that just the two words "Even *you*" all by themselves are an insult. If you try to think of some way to start a sentence with "Even *you*" and finish it without having insulted the person you're speaking to, you'll find it almost impossible. The only examples I can imagine are sorrowful statements of fact in Leveler Mode, such as "Even *you* forgot to write your paper!" in which there is at least a hint that the speaker is surprised that someone like yourself would do that. And it still is far from complimentary.

The basic pattern looks like this:

"Even (X) should (Y)."

ought to
could
would
might
can
may
must
will

That long list of items with "should" at the top is the set of English modal auxiliaries. Like "even," they pack an astonishing amount of information into a very small space. We'll come back to them shortly, but first let's look at some likely fillers for (X) and (Y):

"Even *you*

- a *woman*
- a seventh-*grader*
- a *plumber*
- someone *your* age
- someone who doesn't *care* about his appearance
- a *sophomore*
- an *uneducated* person
- a second *lieutenant*

. . . should [or other modal] . . .

- be able to understand the basic facts of life."
- appreciate the fact that money doesn't grow on trees."
- know that term papers have to be typed."

Your Personal Octagon

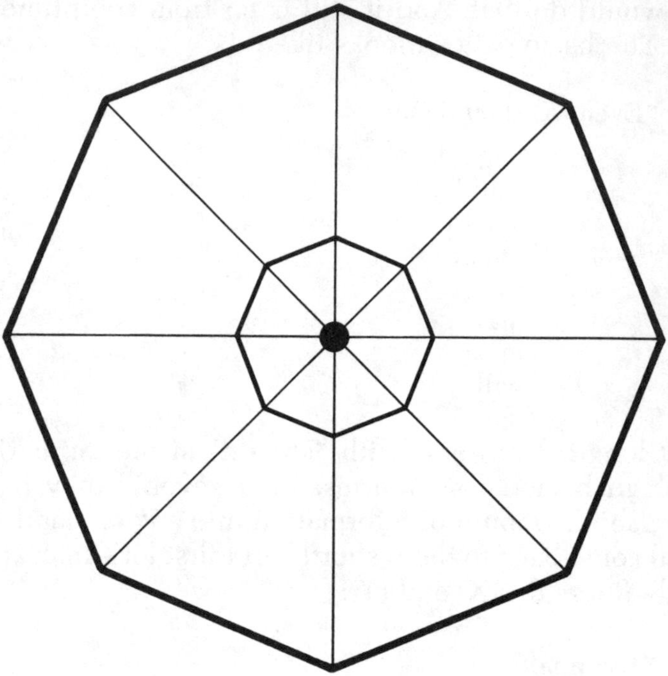

© Suzette Haden Elgin 1978

- realize that being fat is unhealthy."
- be willing to put *some* effort into this job."
- be able to remember that other people have rights, to

Next let's pick one combined example and analyze it for its presuppositions.

> "Even someone *your* age should know that term papers have to be typed."

This sentence has at least the following relevant presuppositions:

1. Whatever your age is, there's something wrong with being that age—it's not an age to be proud of.
2. The fact that term papers have to be typed is so well known that for you not to know it is further proof of how inferior you are.
3. You should feel very guilty and ashamed.

The worst possible response to this is of course to take the bait—whatever was used to fill (Y)—and begin discussing term papers and the typing of term papers. Absolute losing responses go like this:

- "I always type my papers! But my typewriter broke, and it was Sunday, and there was no way to get it fixed, and the paper was due today, and today is Monday!" (This will earn you a chilly lecture about waiting till the very last minute to type your papers, learning to plan ahead so that you never find yourself in a bind like that, and so on forever.)
- "I don't see why they have to be typed as long as they are neat and easy to read." (You can't win this, because it is the teacher who sets up the requirements for paper format, not you. You are in the position of a speeder arguing with a policeman about what the speed limit ought to be.)
- "You never *said* they had to be typed!" (Oops. If you want to be stomped on, this is certainly a good way to guarantee it. The response will be, "The reason I did not say that they had to be typed is because—as I have already pointed out to you—even someone *your* age should know that term papers have to be typed." Not only was it necessary to attack you verbally, you see, but it had to be done *twice*, in *duplicate*, in order to get through to you—and you helped. Please don't do this. You can be absolutely positive that although you may not have known about whatever it was that filled the [Y] slot, it *is* something your opponent can get away with claiming that you have no excuse not to know about. If it weren't something like that, it wouldn't

be appearing in this pattern. You are never going to hear a sentence like this one, in which [Y] is filled by something likely to be known only to specialists: "Even someone *your* age should know that Mount Erebus is just over thirteen-thousand feet high.")

The first step in dealing with a Section D move is to ignore the bait and identify the presuppositions; then respond to them, not to the bait. Look at this sample confrontation:

CONFRONTATION EIGHT

Husband: Even a *woman* ought to be able to change a flat tire, you know.

Wife: I *can* change a flat tire, and just as well as any man, too.

Husband: Sweetheart, there's no need for that tone of voice, or that look on your face. Just because I want to be sure you don't find yourself stuck out on some highway in the middle of nowhere.

Wife: Now wait just a minute, here. What exactly do you mean by "that tone of voice" and "that look on your face" anyway? You started this, you know.

Husband: [With a look of total amazement] I started *what?*

WIFE here has no hope whatsoever and will very shortly be told at some length about how impossible it is to talk to her about anything, how touchy she is, how she blows up over every little thing and imagines that HUSBAND is trying to pick fights. And then she will be apologizing and saying that she simply doesn't know what on earth is wrong with her. This is the Valium Trail, Beginner's Slope.

WIFE should go to Computer Mode, respond to the presupposition, and maintain her stance, like this:

> *Husband:* Even a *woman* ought to be able to change a flat tire, you know.
>
> *Wife:* The opinion that women are somehow inferior to men is a rather common one—but I'm surprised to hear it coming from you, darling.

This is a nonviolent thing to say and should leave HUSBAND with some intricate maneuvering to do. It is gentle and ends with a compliment, presupposing that HUSBAND is not the sort of unsatisfactory person who would have said what he just said and that it must have been a slip. Perhaps *he* is not quite himself lately.

If a counterattack cannot be avoided, it goes this way:

> *Wife:* The opinion that women are somehow inferior to men is a rather common one in men your age, darling—it's nothing to be concerned about.

The crucial sequence is the phrase "in men your age," which can be filled in with anything to which you know this person is vulnerable. If you have no idea, there is the all-purpose filler "a rather common one in men in your situation"; after all, *he* knows what his situation is, and there is sure to be something about it that worries him. He will fill in the missing piece for you.

The essential pattern of response to a Section D attack is a complicated-looking arrangement:

> "The opinion that . . . [*fill in whatever is presupposed by (X)*] . . . is a rather . . . [*fill in with an appropriate adjective—'common,' 'interesting,' 'typical'*.] . . . one, but I am surprised to hear it from you."

Now I want to return to the modal auxiliaries, as promised. They are very important in verbal self-defense, and they include the following: "can," "could," "should," "will," "would," "may," "might," "must," "shall" (very rare in American English). The auxiliary "should" often surfaces as "ought to."

The modals have several functions in English. One of them is to let a speaker carry out what is called a speech *act,* such as a command. This isn't the function we're interested in, but to make the distinction clear, look at the following pair of sentences:

- "John must leave."
- "John must have left."

The first is a kind of command, ordering John to leave; the second is only a statement of the speaker's opinion, and it is this function that concerns us. The modals allow a speaker to state an opinion or make a comment about all the rest of the sentence in which they appear. If we had to make this at least roughly explicit for "John must have left" we would get a strange and pedantic utterance, something like this:

> "I the speaker, based upon all the knowledge and evidence available to me at this moment, hereby state that it is my opinion that John is no longer here."

It would be both boring and awkward to have to go through all that every time we wanted to express what the modals express, and that makes them extremely useful. They are small paragraphs, handily squashed into a single word. But by the same token, because they have so much content that is not obvious on the surface, it is important to learn to pay close attention to them. For example:

- "You must leave" PRESUPPOSES that the speaker has the authority or the power to decide whether you stay or not.
- "You should leave" PRESUPPOSES almost the same thing as

"must"—only kings and queens say, "You *shall* leave"—but does so more subtly, and is therefore the most common modal in a Section D attack. It says something like this: "Although I the speaker am not so arrogant as to actually give you an order, based upon the knowledge and evidence that I now have, it is clear that I have the right to suggest that you leave; and it is very polite of me to put it this way instead of just telling you to get out of here."

That is a *lot* of buried content. If you accept it all without protest, you may find that you've set a precedent which will return to cause you much trouble later. Pay attention to the modals; they are always important. Here is a brief run-through of their presuppositions, without quite so much elaboration, in order to clarify them. (Assume that each begins with "I the speaker hereby state that . . . ")

Stated.		*Presupposed.*
"John	can leave."	"John is able to leave."
"John	could leave."	"John is able to leave if certain conditions are met."
"John	should leave."	"It would be desirable for John to leave."
"John	will leave."	"John is certain to leave."
"John	would leave."	"John's leaving could be predicted with certainty if certain conditions were met."
"John	may leave."	"It's possible that John will leave."
"John	might leave."	"It's possible that John will leave."
"John	must leave."	"It's necessary for John to leave."

(The distinction between "may" and "might" is disappearing from contemporary American English.)

People frequently soften the effect of their modals by putting a question after them, like this:

"You should leave, don't you think?"

What this does is express your opinion at the same time that it offers the person you're speaking to equal rights to their own opinion, thus canceling out the relationship of dominance and turning a concealed command into a slightly more neutral utterance.

Now try the practice confrontations for this chapter.

CONFRONTATION NINE

Patient: Even a *nurse* ought to be able to tell that I'm really in a lot of pain!

Nurse: ______________________________

____

____

Patient: ______________________________

____

____

Nurse: ______________________________

____

____

(Who won?)

CONFRONTATION TEN

Friend 1: Even someone who really has no interest at all in the feelings of other people should be willing to make an effort *once* in a while!

Friend 2: ______________________________

____

____

Friend 1: ______________________________

____

____

Friend 2: ______________________________

____

____

(Who won?)

YOUR JOURNAL
SECTION D ATTACKS ON ME:

(1) Date ______________________________

____

Situation ______________________________

____

____

FIRST MOVE - What My Opponent Said ______________

____

____

____

What I Said ______________________________

____

____

____

What I Should Have Said ______________________

____

____

____

SECOND MOVE - What My Opponent Said __________

____

____

____

What I Said ______________________________

____

____

____

What I Should Have Said ____________________

____

____

____

THIRD MOVE - What My Opponent Said __________

____

____

____

____

What I Said ______________________________

____

____

____

What I Should Have Said ____________________

____

____

____

FOURTH MOVE - What My Opponent Said ________

____

____

What I Said

What I Should Have Said

(2) Date

Situation

FIRST MOVE - What My Opponent Said

What I Said

What I Should Have Said ____________________

____

____

____

SECOND MOVE - What My Opponent Said __________

____

____

____

What I Said ______________________________

____

____

____

What I Should Have Said ____________________

____

____

____

THIRD MOVE - What My Opponent Said ___________

____

____

____

What I said ______________________________

____

____

What I Should Have Said ____________________

____

____

____

FOURTH MOVE - What My Opponent Said __________

____

____

____

What I said ____________________________

____

____

____

What I Should Have Said ____________________

____

____

SAMPLE SCRIPTS

CONFRONTATION NINE

Patient: Even a *nurse* ought to be able to tell that I'm really in a lot of pain!

Nurse: You know, it's astonishing how many people still feel, after all these years, that nurses have no training at all. What do you suppose accounts for that?

Patient: *Do* nurses have a lot of training?

Nurse: Well, first we have to finish four whole years of

undergraduate work—and lots of times it takes five because of extra requirements. And then we have to pass state examinations.

NURSE is handling this very well; and with a patient who is in pain, winning and losing is not relevant. The point is to reassure PATIENT, who may actually be afraid that NURSE doesn't know how to do anything but fill out charts and stick people with needles and who wants a doctor at once. If the patient *is* in pain (and the proper assumption should be that he or she is, until there is evidence to the contrary), NURSE is also helping with that problem. Distracting PATIENT with an abstract discussion of nursing training is useful here. If, while he or she is talking to PATIENT, NURSE is also having to do unpleasant things with tubes or needles or other medical apparatus, all distraction is to the good.

Patient: Even a *nurse* ought to be able to tell that I'm really in a lot of pain!

Nurse: There's nothing wrong with being a nurse, sir. Nurses are skilled professionals.

Patient: Oh, yeah? I came in here hurting like the devil, and what you're doing hurts worse than what I came in with, and you either call a doctor right now or I'm walking out of this place before one of you "professionals" finishes me off!

Nurse: You're free to leave if you like, sir, but I do *not* have to listen to any more of your insults, and I don't intend to.

This is an unfortunate mess. People who are sick and in pain are not at their most reasonable to begin with, and nurses assuredly do know that. This nurse is now engaged in an undignified and unprofessional row with a patient;

and whether the patient deserves it or not is unimportant. It need never have happened.

NURSE was correct to respond to the presupposition—that being a nurse is somehow second-rate, something to be ashamed of. But NURSE has forgotten to respond with a *neutral* question or remark; there is nothing neutral about the move made in response to the Section D attack. If the patient does not happen to be a "skilled professional" himself, it has gone beyond the level of non-neutrality and become an insult. Bad form, and nowhere to go but downhill. PATIENT will complain about this nurse, no matter how skillful and efficient the care provided, and the already low opinion PATIENT has of nurses in general has now been given a strong reinforcement that will be no help in the future.

Patient: Even a *nurse* ought to be able to tell that I'm really in a lot of pain!

Nurse: Ma'am, have you always thought that nurses didn't really know what they were doing?

Patient: Look, are you insinuating that I was trying to insult you? Because if you were, you've picked the wrong person to try that on!

Nurse: Ma'am, I was only trying to help. If I've offended you, I'm sorry.

This is an example of using more force than the situation requires—the question NURSE asks is not really neutral. It comes too close to accusing PATIENT of having said that nurses don't know what they're doing. PATIENT is in pain and may be frightened as well; furthermore, she appears to be somewhat touchy. For NURSE to switch to Placater Mode in an attempt to correct the mistake is only going to increase PATIENT's lack of confidence.

It is a good idea to remember that most people who begin with "Even a *nurse*" are not contrasting nurses with all other possible sets of individuals in the universe. Usually what is meant is "Even a nurse" as compared with a doctor. The traditional mystique that has doctors carrying the power of life and death and nurses carrying bedpans is something that patients may not be aware they feel. It is strongly reinforced by the images of doctors and nurses on television, in movies, and in written materials, starting with the first reading text in elementary school in which the nurse is always a respectful female doing minor things in attendance on a forceful male doctor who is doing *important* things. Any nurse is going to have to contend with this, and it might just as well be looked upon as one of Life's Burdens, along with heavy traffic, bad weather, taxes, diaper rash, and whatever else you want to put on the list. Being defensive about it will not help matters, even though it may be wholly justified.

Patient: Even a *nurse* ought to be able to tell that I'm really in a lot of pain!

Nurse: You're absolutely right, and I'm going to do something about it just as quickly as possible.

Patient: I'm sorry . . . I guess I'm not being very pleasant.

Nurse: Anybody who is in pain is likely to be a little bit on edge. No problem.

In this example NURSE has ignored the fact that PATIENT's opening utterance contained an insulting presupposition and has agreed with it as if it had been made neutrally. (Whether a particular patient deserves this sort of treatment or is a chronically abusive one who needs no further encouragement of bad habits is a decision that has to be made for each individual case.) PATIENT has reacted well, and NURSE has not rubbed PATIENT's nose in the apology. The immediate switch by NURSE in the second move from the individual PATIENT to the abstract "anybody who is in pain" is an easy way to accomplish this. To have said back, "Oh, the only reason you insulted me is because you are in pain, and I don't pay any attention to that kind of thing" would have been a much inferior way of going about this. It would smack of "Me, Noble Professional; You, Primitive Patient." NURSE has demonstrated considerable skill by the speed with which the focus of the confrontation was removed from the already embarrassed PATIENT and placed on an abstraction.

CONFRONTATION TEN

Friend 1: Even someone who really has no interest at all in the feelings of other people should be willing to make an effort *once* in a while!

Friend 2: When did you start thinking I don't have any interest in other people's feelings?

Friend 1: You *don't*. It's obvious to anybody. You just don't care about anything but yourself!

Friend 2: Like I said, when did you start feeling this way?

FRIEND 1 here is determined to remain in Blamer Mode and is not going to be distracted by FRIEND 2's neutral question. Whatever it is that's bothering FRIEND 1 is going to have to be brought out in the open eventually, and all FRIEND 2 can do is hang in there. The chances are about 9 to 1 in a confrontation like this that shortly—if FRIEND 2 can remain calm and in Computer Mode—FRIEND 1 will bring up a specific incident: a forgotten birthday, a remark overheard somewhere or repeated to FRIEND 1 by someone else and interpreted as an insult, something that has been festering and needs to be talked out. The goal, if you value the friendship, should be to work this into a Leveler Mode so that you and FRIEND 2 can get to the bottom of the matter and be rid of it.

Friend 1: Even someone who really has no interest at all

in the feelings of other people should be willing to make an effort *once* in a while!

Friend 2: When did you start thinking I don't have any interest in other people's feelings?

Friend 1: Yesterday. When I needed you in that meeting, and you just sat there and watched me go down the tubes.

Friend 2: Want to get some coffee and talk about it?

FRIEND 2, if he or she is paying close attention, will have a temptation to fight off here. The bait in this Section D has a presupposition that FRIEND 1 *never* makes an effort to consider other people's feelings. Then here comes this single incident from only yesterday, and the temptation will be strong to say something like "I thought you said I *never* . . ." and so on. If you do that, however, FRIEND 1 will begin dredging up other incidents, valid or ridiculous, and you'll be into a Blamer-Blamer confrontation, headed nowhere. Resist the temptation and try to make the one incident the subject of your conversation.

If your invitation for coffee and talk is turned down, what do you do? Just say, "Okay," and let it go. There'll be another time to mend the fences if you want to mend them. Do not Placate and beg FRIEND 2—one invitation to Level is quite enough.

Friend 1: Even someone who really has no interest at all in the feelings of other people should be willing to make an effort *once* in a while!

Friend 2: Why do you suppose you think I don't have any interest in other people's feelings?

Friend 1: Because of the way you act.

Friend 2: For instance . . .

Again, you are after a specific and concrete incident

to discuss, instead of this vast general accusation, and you are doing it properly. Be careful of body language and intonation here, however. If you sound belligerent with your "For instance," if you come across like a child saying, "Name me just one time, just one time, I dare you!" It's not going to work. The goal is a neutral discussion, and Computer Mode (both verbal and nonverbal) is indicated. Be sure that you do not end the "For instance" with a question mark—"For instance?" Let the phrase fall casually and wait.

Friend 1: Even someone who really has no interest at all in the feelings of other people should be willing to make an effort *once* in a while!

Friend 2: Have you always felt that way about me? *I* thought we were *friends!*

Friend 1: If we weren't friends, would I be bothering with this?

Friend 2: Well, if it's such a bother, *don't!* I don't need your comments on my character, thanks.

This is what happens when, after asking your question in response to a presupposition, you cannot resist throwing in a little bit extra. FRIEND 2 might get back "We *are* friends, and no, I haven't always felt this way," and so on into a productive discussion. On the other hand, things may go as in the example, and by throwing out that bait—"*I* thought we were *friends!*"—FRIEND 2 leaves himself or herself wide open for escalation of the attack. Be sure it's worth the risk before you do this sort of thing. Notice the presuppositions in the tag line. FRIEND 1 will hear, "I thought we were friends, but obviously I was mistaken and you're not my friend at all." It's the heavy stress on "I" and "friends" that guarantees that.

Section E Attacks

Everyone Understands Why You . . .

8

There are two basic patterns for the Section E attack. The first uses the undefined term "everyone" and looks like this:

> "Everyone understands why you (X)."

Possible items to fill the (X) are like these:

> "Everyone understands why you
> - are so emotional."
> - are so confused."
> - are so hysterical."

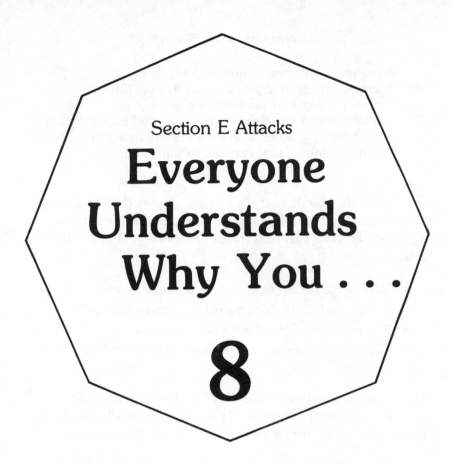

- really haven't been yourself lately."
- are convinced that you have a physical illness."
- cannot bring your sales up to normal."
- really cannot function adequately in a Ph.D. program."
- are having so much trouble adjusting to military life. (to life in the dorms; to this class; to your marriage.)"

The other basic pattern simply makes the "everyone" more specific, replacing it with a sequence that applies to a particular group and includes the person spoken to, like this:

- "All the other members of the staff understand . . . "
- "Every student in this program understands . . . "
- "Every nurse on this floor understands . . . "
- "All of the men/women who have to work with you understand . . . "

This opening is then followed by the items in (X), as in the more simple pattern. It is also possible to throw modals into the mix, giving us such monstrosities as

> "No one in this department with even a shred of common decency could possibly fail to understand why you are having so much trouble meeting our standards, Ms./Mr. Smith."

Here we have presuppositions piled and stacked and coming out of the woodwork. This is not a beginner's move, and it can be extremely difficult to handle. This is particularly true because it usually comes at you in a situation in which you have been called in to face the other person in isolation, and in which that other person can easily set up a surface facade of tender, loving concern for you by the bucket—yet it is really an attack, and is

Your Personal Octagon

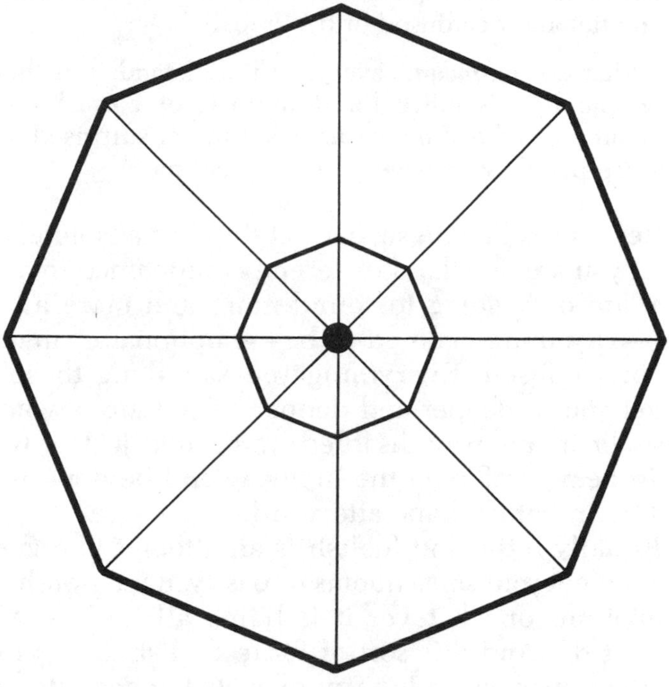

© Suzette Haden Elgin 1978

often a vicious one. The Section E attack is likely to leave a beginner feeling beaten and bewildered and resentful, and absolutely unable to understand why he or she has reacted so strangely to this person who has just been so *kind.*

From your work with the earlier sections of the Octagon, it will be apparent to you that the bait—the part to be ignored—is what appears on the surface, filling the (X) slot in the pattern. You do not, under any circumstances, want to make replies like these:

"Anybody who is saying that I am emotional is completely out of line, and I want that understood. In no *way* am I emotional [or confused or hysterical]."

"What do you *mean,* 'everyone understands'? If there are people in this office [or dormitory, or barracks] talking about me and calling me names, I'm not surprised; but it's those people who have problems, not me."

Responses like these, even if they are absolutely true, even if you are an island of serene competence in a sea of chaos, are only going to sound more and more as if you were—as you are claimed to be—emotional or unable to cope or confused. Everything you say along these lines will get you in deeper and deeper; if you are a woman or elderly or in any way disabled, you might just as well go play in heavy traffic on the highway and be done with it: You'd be in better shape afterward.

Equally futile and foolish is an attempt to argue that you *can* meet your sales quotas or pass your comprehensive examinations or whatever it is being alleged in (X) that you can't do. And this sort of futile foolishness is exactly what the person attacking you expects to encounter.

The real danger of a Section E is in these presuppositions:

- "There is something very wrong with you."
- "This 'something wrong' is well known to everyone around you."
- "This something wrong is *so* wrong that we are all more than willing to forgive you for (X)."
- "You should be very, very grateful to all of us for being so perceptive and so understanding."
- "You should be very, very ashamed of yourself."

Personally I would rather be socked once than have

all this dumped on me and not know how to handle it. The child who begs to be spanked rather than lectured to understands this quite clearly.

Remember, on pages 35, 54, and 91, the counterattacks that were described for emergency use only? Remember the discussion on page 91 of ways to proceed when you don't know precisely where your opponent is vulnerable? Section E attacks are based upon this same mechanism, which is one of the fundamental truths:

> Everybody in the whole world has *something* he or she looks upon as a dirty little secret and would hate for anybody else to know about.

Anyone using these moves, even with no idea at all what your particular hidden-away and gnawed-over secret is, can count on the fact that *you* know or think you know. And they can count on your reacting to "a person in your situation" or to "Everyone understands why you (X)" with this thought: "Oh, no! Everybody knows about *IT!*"

It's most unlikely that they know about your personal IT. I assure you, that's true. Whether it is your sexual preferences or the fact that you once stole three dollars from petty cash and have never put it back; whether it is that you are a bigamist or were arrested nine years ago for participating in a political demonstration or running a red light and have been lying about that; whether, as in the vast majority of people I come across, it is only a feeling that your thighs are lumpy or that you're too short, it makes no difference. True, if you've done something really awful and done it blatantly, it may have come to light. But usually that has not happened. Usually the person using a Section E is simply counting on you to fill in the secret IT from your personal knowledge and fall apart about it. That is what ordinarily happens.

I have seen a student, once or twice, fall right into this trap and blurt out something like "Oh, no! How did you find out that I cheated on that test?" even though the instructor had never suspected anything of the kind. Don't do that, please. If you have something to confess, the time for confessing may come along later, and you may have a moral decision to make about that. But this is *not* the time. Not yet. Not when you don't know what you're up against.

Which leads us to what you *can* safely do. There is a beginner's move that has a high safety factor and requires little effort. It will come as a great surprise to your attacker.

> *Other Person:* Everyone understands why you (X).
>
> *You:* How very kind of them. I'm deeply touched.

A response of this kind leaves your attacker in a curious position—if you do it properly; that is, if you sound sincere, calm, and mildly interested in what is coming next. You have now presupposed, you see, that you and the attacker and all the members of the mysterious "everyone" (or specified group) share your secret. And if this person you're dealing with is working from ignorance, as is typical, he or she is going to have the communication problem now, not you. This defense is one you can memorize, just as you memorized "Pardon me" for when you bumped into somebody. Use it, and then sit back and wait, looking calm, and *mildly* interested.

More advanced elaborations of this defense are responses such as the following:

> "The company [or dormitory, or therapy group, or whatever] that is able to achieve a spirit of community such as that evidenced by what you have just said to me is undoubtedly rare, and a credit to your leadership. One can

only feel sympathy for other groups in which that spirit is lacking."

You'll recognize this as straight Computer Mode, as a response not to the bait but to the presuppositions, as a complete denial that you feel or should feel any guilt (or any gratitude) other than a kind of neutrally polite appreciation of "their" good manners; and it is very hard to follow it up with something nasty back at you. Furthermore, you will recognize it as a move away from the personal and dangerous one-on-one situation that opened the exchange to a much safer discussion of an abstract issue—that is, the "spirit of community" and its various ramifications. (If "spirit of community" is not appropriate, by the way, insert whatever chunk of jargon does fit your situation.)

Your attacker has of course been complimented at great length. What may amaze you is how much of this you can lay on, and how thickly you can lay it on, without it being recognized for the shuck it is. People in power, especially if they enjoy using Section E moves, can swallow an incredible amount of this sort of thing if you keep it in Computer Mode. How far you want to carry it depends on how strong your own stomach is and how skilled you are at judging your opponent's limits. The example seems to me to go about as far as you should either need or want to go. However, it's important for you to be aware that the reaction to your remarks is not as likely to be that you are toadying as you would think. The Section E user is often almost lusting to hear about his or her great abilities as a leader, or potential as a scholar or administrator.

I want to introduce one concept here, very briefly, because it is such an important characteristic of Computer Mode and has been used in the expanded defense move in this chapter. It's called the *nominalization,* and its function in verbal encounters is to hide away what is actually being said. Obviously, for you to say to the Section E attacker, flatly and baldly, "You are a great leader," would be sickening. It wouldn't work, despite what you see happening in television situation comedies. (At least I hope it wouldn't; I hope nobody is that naïve and still in a position to use Section E's on you.) But you do want to slip that remark in there, where Ms./Mr. Jones will hear it without quite realizing where it came from. You do that by nominalization. Look at these following examples:

1. a. "The students • cheated on their final exam."
   b. "The students' cheating on their final exam • distressed the entire faculty."
2. a. "Elizabeth • is careless with her children."
   b. "Elizabeth's carelessness with her children • must have some reasonable explanation."
3. a. "Bob • is cruel to animals."
   b. "Bob's cruelty to animals • is something that none of us who know and admire him can understand."

In each of the (a) examples a flat statement has been made, an open and overt claim. It appears in the predicate* of the utterance (to the right of the dot), and the burden of its proof is on the speaker. Anyone listening can legitimately demand that proof. In the (b) examples, however, the only claims being made on the surface are those that appear in the predicates, and they are things that are not likely to outrage the listener. The *hidden* claims have been nominalized and moved into the subject of the sentence, where they are now only presupposed. That is,

* In English, the term "predicate" covers a wide range of things, including verbs and adjectives.

"The students cheated" presupposes that the students exist and claims openly that they cheated. "The students' cheating distressed the faculty" *presupposes* the existence of the cheating and claims only that it distressed the faculty. This is an ancient technique of the political speech, the propaganda message, and the sales pitch, and you need to recognize it when it's coming at you, even if it goes by very fast.

Nominalization means only turning a "verby" thing into a "nouny" thing. Some verby things have special forms for this process in English. For example:

careful		carefulness
abandon		abandonment
patriotic	*becomes*	patriotism
resign		resignation

Any item can be nominalized, however, just by adding "-ing" and, in most cases, a possessive marker of some kind. The examples that follow should make this clear:

4. a. Bill • burned down the building.
   b. Bill's burning down the building • was unfortunate.
5. a. He • smokes.
   b. His smoking • came as a surprise to me.
6. a. For anybody to cheat • is unwise.
   b. Cheating • is unwise.

In example 6(b) you will notice that there is no possessive marker, such as "Bill's" or "his." The person or persons doing the cheating have been eliminated from the utterance completely, and the abstract *action*—cheating—appears as the nominalization. This is Computer Mode at its most advanced and is used frequently to create symbols either to rally round or protest against, as the case may be.

The more nominalizations you are able to use in Computer Mode, or *any* mode, the more chunks of meaning you will be able to hide away as presuppositions. In Computer Mode it should almost never be necessary for you to make *any* open claim that could be objected to; that is why Computers never seem to take a stand on any issue. They constantly nominalize and then tack on a completely innocuous predicate. This is a technique to be practiced until you feel absolutely at ease with it and something you should watch for until it is impossible for anyone to slip a nominalization past you unnoticed.

Here are your sample confrontations for this chapter. In working with them, try to use nominalizations whenever they can be fit in.

CONFRONTATION ELEVEN

(Note: For this particular exercise, assume that the "secret" worrying the employee, a part-time saleswoman, is her personal conviction that she is overweight and that other people perceive her as being fat.)

Employer: Dear, everyone understands why you are having so much difficulty finding a place for yourself in this job. We really *do* understand.

Employee: ____________________________________

____

____

Employer: ____________________________________

____

____

Employee: ______________________________________

____

____

(Who won?)

CONFRONTATION TWELVE
(Note: Try approaching this exercise with different combinations of gender for *Doctor* and *Patient* in mind.)

Doctor: I want you to know that every one of the doctors you have seen—and that includes myself—understands why you are so convinced that you have a physical disease instead of an emotional problem.

Patient: ______________________________________

____

____

Doctor: ______________________________________

____

____

Patient: ______________________________________

____

____

(Who won?)

YOUR JOURNAL
SECTION E ATTACKS ON ME:

(1) Date ______________________________

Situation ______________________________

____

FIRST MOVE - What My Opponent Said ______________

____

____

What I Said ______________________________

____

____

What I Should Have Said ______________________

____

____

SECOND MOVE - What My Opponent Said ___________

____

____

What I Said ______________________________

____

____

What I Should Have Said ______________________

____

____

THIRD MOVE - What My Opponent Said ____________

____

____

What I Said ________________________________

____

____

What I Should Have Said ____________________

____

____

FOURTH MOVE - What My Opponent Said ________

____

____

What I Said ________________________________

____

____

What I Should Have Said ____________________

____

____

(2) Date ____________________________________

Situation ______________________________

____

FIRST MOVE - What My Opponent Said ___________

____

What I Said ______________________________

____

____

What I Should Have Said ____________________

____

____

SECOND MOVE - What My Opponent Said __________

____

____

What I Said ______________________________

____

____

What I Should Have Said ____________________

____

____

THIRD MOVE - What My Opponent Said ___________

____

____

What I Said ______________________________

____

____

What I Should Have Said ____________________

____

____

FOURTH MOVE - What My Opponent Said __________

____

____

What I Said ____________________________

____

____

What I Should Have Said __________________

____

____

SAMPLE SCRIPTS

CONFRONTATION ELEVEN

Employer: Dear, everyone understands why you are having so much difficulty finding a place for yourself in this job. We really *do* understand.

Employee: How kind of everyone. I appreciate their concern.

Employer: Well, it includes me, too, you know. *I* understand, *too.*

Employee: It's certainly gratifying to know that.

This is properly done. Now EMPLOYER is going to have to come right out and say what it is that "everyone" understands or else take another tack entirely. And EM-

PLOYEE should do *nothing* to help EMPLOYER out of this bind.

Employer: Dear, everyone understands why you are having so much difficulty finding a place for yourself in this job. We really *do* understand.

Employee: That's not at all surprising. The team spirit here is obvious, and something for which you are to be congratulated.

Employer: Well, thank you. . . . I appreciate that.

Employee: Not at all. I believe in giving credit where it is due.

Having been complimented three times in succession, EMPLOYER is going to sound foolish if the next move is an accusation or a complaint. So far, EMPLOYEE is winning.

Employer: Dear, everyone understands why you are having so much difficulty finding a place for yourself in this job. We really *do* understand.

Employee: Just because I'm fat, Ms. O'Donahue, does *not* mean that I can't handle my job. Fat people are just like any other kind of people—they're a little larger, that's all.

Employer: *Really,* dear, if you are so sensitive about your weight—to the extent that you let it interfere with your job performance—don't you think you should pull yourself together and go on a diet?

Employee: I have *tried* that. I've tried every diet that was every invented, and they do no good at all. That's not the point! The point is that accusing me of being no good at my job just because I'm fat is unfair.

This is a disaster. For one thing, EMPLOYEE has now given EMPLOYER the full details about where to jab if she wants to hurt her, something that EMPLOYER may not have had any suspicion of up to this point. For another, EMPLOYEE is now wide open for a new attack: "If you *really* wanted to lose weight, you'd be able to," and all that goes with that. If EMPLOYER is looking for a perfect victim, she has found one.

Employer: Dear, everyone understands why you are having so much difficulty finding a place for yourself in this job. We really *do* understand.

Employee: How perceptive of them—and how nice of you to mention it.

Employer: Well . . . that's not really what I wanted to talk to you about.

Employee: Oh, sorry. Nothing like a misunderstanding to start off a conversation! Why don't we start over?

EMPLOYEE has done this very well and is now in as much command of the situation as is possible, given the fact that she is the employee and has little in the way of power to use. If EMPLOYER now moves to straight Blamer Mode and starts criticizing EMPLOYEE's job performance—which is likely—she will do so on a footing of less dominance and will have to lay her cards on the table. No matter how things go, this is a few points for EMPLOYEE. Notice, too, that by using the nominalization "a misunderstanding," EMPLOYEE has carefully avoided any claim as to who misunderstood whom. This is an ingenious touch.

CONFRONTATION TWELVE

(In the examples that follow, all possible combinations of gender have been used for DOCTOR and PATIENT. This is because the gender difference in the DOCTOR-PATIENT situation has such a drastic effect upon the entire confrontation.)

Doctor (male): I want you to know, Miriam, that every one of the doctors you have seen—and that includes myself—understands why you are so convinced that you have a physical disease instead of an emotional problem.

Patient: Do they? I'm sure the support of one's peers is always reassuring in situations of this kind, Doctor.

Doctor: I'm not sure you understood what I was trying to say to you, Miriam.

Patient: That is of course possible. [PATIENT waits with an expression of neutral interest.]

In this situation you cannot, as PATIENT, express your gratitude or appreciation for DOCTOR's statement, no matter how many other doctors agree with him. Since you don't agree, that would be absurd and would reinforce his conviction that you have emotional problems. PATIENT here is probably at a number of disadvantages: For example, DOCTOR is dressed, while PATIENT is either naked or wearing a paper gown; DOCTOR is addressed by title, while PATIENT gets first-name treatment; DOCTOR is male, PATIENT is female; and so on. Under the circumstances, PATIENT is well advised to go to Computer Mode and attempt to adjust the unequal dominance situation a bit, and that is what she has done. DOCTOR is going to have to be a good deal more specific.

Doctor (male): I want you to know, Harry, that every one of the doctors you have seen—and that includes myself—understands why you are so convinced that you have a physical disease instead of an emotional problem.

Patient: The way that doctors are always able to agree on every issue is an amazing phenomenon. One wonders what the medical profession would be like without that determination to hang together at all costs.

Doctor: Oh, I think that impression of doctors is very much exaggerated.

Patient: Hmmmm. Interesting.

So far, PATIENT is way out in front. DOCTOR has just questioned the idea that the consensus opinion of a group of doctors is necessarily inevitable, which is some distance away from the question of whether PATIENT's problem is physical or emotional. It is now DOCTOR's move, and he will either have to pursue this unrelated topic, or retrace his moves and begin again, or choose some totally different strategy. PATIENT has maintained Computer Mode throughout the entire exchange and is in a strong position.

Doctor (female): I want you to know, Miriam, that every one of the doctors you have seen—and that includes myself—understands why you are so convinced that you have a physical disease instead of an emotional problem.

Patient: That's to be expected, under the circumstances; it would be unrealistic to anticipate a *lack* of agreement."

Doctor: You're not surprised, then?

Patient: If you *expected* me to be surprised, Doctor, I *am* surprised. Perhaps I misunderstood your first remark.

PATIENT is doing very well here. They are fencing, she and DOCTOR, and where this may lead is impossible to predict. However, the first response PATIENT made, with the phrase "under the circumstances," was an excellent move. DOCTOR has presupposed that everyone (that is, the set of doctors PATIENT has seen) knows something about PATIENT, which justifies the claim that is being made. PATIENT has replied with an utterance presupposing that she knows something, too, and can at least hope that DOCTOR is wondering what it is.

Doctor (female): I want you to know, Harry, that every one of the doctors you have seen—and that includes myself—understands why you are so convinced that you have a physical disease instead of an emotional problem.

Patient: Yeah? Well, I want *you* to know, Doctor, that I am damned sick and tired of hearing that. I've heard it from ten men who called themselves doctors, and I thought from a woman doctor I might at least get a different opening *line,* for crying out loud. Thanks for nothing, Doctor.

Doctor: Harry, try to listen to me reasonably, would you? I'm *not* saying you're not sick, and I'm *not* saying your pain isn't real; and neither are the other doctors. We're simply trying to tell you that the problem you have is not the kind of thing that can be helped by *medicine.*

Patient: And I am saying that you're all wrong, Doctor. And if I have to go to a hundred doctors before I find one that knows something, I will.

PATIENT is losing, of course, and can't win. It makes no difference whether he is right or wrong about his condition. He may very well be sitting there with a genuine organic disease that can and should be treated medically—for example, a gallbladder that ought to be removed. It doesn't matter. His verbal behavior in this confrontation is only going to reinforce DOCTOR'S image of him as an overemotional person with little self-control who trudges from doctor to doctor in search of one who will agree with his personal diagnosis. That may be unjust, and even dangerous to PATIENT, but it is the way things are.

Doctor-Patient confrontations are rather special, because of the privileged position and status that physicians have in American society, and because—unlike the situation in most confrontations—the doctor often has the power of life and death over the patient. This tends to make the confrontations highly charged with overtones that would be absent in almost any other setting.

Section F Attacks

A Person Who . . .

9

The Section F move has an absurdly trivial-looking basic pattern. It goes this:

> "A person who (X) (Y)."

Its danger lies in those characteristics that make it look so boringly simple, that is, that it offers neither restrictions nor information. It is in full Computer Mode, referring to some unknown "person" rather than directly to the listener. And almost anything may be used to fill (X) and (Y), which makes it a versatile attack that can turn up in almost any imaginable situation.

Possible ways to fill the empty (X) are listed below:

"A person who
- really *wanted* to (Z) . . ."
- has serious emotional problems . . ."
- doesn't even *care* about (Z) . . ."
- has limited perceptions . . ."
- always puts other people last . . ."
- has no interest in achieving anything meaningful . . ."

Notice that these are stacked, attack inside attack, and that a new empty slot can be put inside some of them with no difficulty at all. For example, we could fill (Z) in the first example like this:

"A person who really *wanted* to
- get through boot camp . . ."
- be accepted by this fraternity . . ."
- gain weight . . ."
- get well . . ."
- get along with other people . . ."
- pass this course . . ."

Similarly, the other example with a (Z) could be "A person who doesn't even *care* about their grades . . ." and so on.

Now, we can take one example from the lists to serve as the "A person who (X)" section and look at ways of filling term (Y) in the basic pattern.

"A person who really *wanted* to pass this course
- would be careful to *always* arrive in class on time."
- would never turn in a paper that had not been properly researched and immaculately typed."
- would realize that at least six hours of outside work are required for every class meeting and would be willing to put in those hours."
- would not ask a stupid question like that one!"

If we now take just one of these and look at its primary presuppositions, we will (at last) have searched out most of the nooks and crannies of that innocent-looking "A person who (X) (Y)" that we started with. Let's use this sentence:

> "A person who really *wanted* to pass this course would never turn in a paper that had not been properly researched and immaculately typed."

Your Personal Octagon

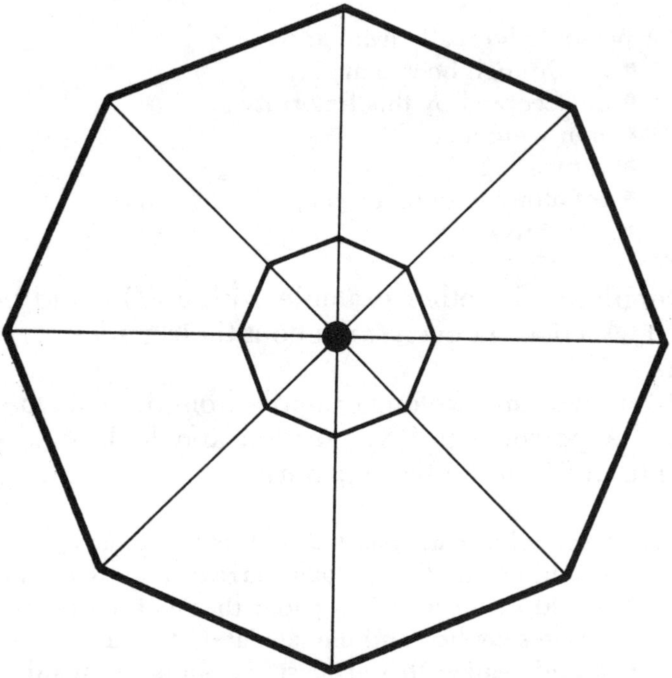

The presuppositions are

- "There is a set of persons who really want to pass this course—and you are not one of that set."
- "Your paper has not been properly researched."
- "Your paper has not been immaculately typed."

The bait is the claim that your paper is badly researched and typed. But an immediate response to that bait, such as

> "Dr. Lopez, I spent almost *six weeks* researching that paper, and it was typed according to the style sheet you specified for this class yourself!"

is even more stupid than usual. You, personally, have *not* been openly accused by Dr. Lopez, who can be counted on to inform you of that fact like this:

> "*Mr.* Martin—I do not recall having even mentioned your paper, your research, or your typing."

This statement is accurate and will make you look both conceited and foolish. Let's put this one through a few more moves.

CONFRONTATION THIRTEEN

Dr. Lopez: A person who really *wanted* to pass this course would never turn in a paper that had not been properly researched and immaculately typed.

Student: Dr. Lopez, I spent almost *six weeks* researching that paper, and it was typed according to the style sheet you specified for this class yourself!

Dr. Lopez: *Mr.* Martin—I do not recall having even mentioned your paper, your research, or your typing.

Student: But that's what you *meant!* I mean, you may

not have said it right out in so many words, but that *is* what you *meant!*

Dr. Lopez: It is astonishing how many students one encounters who are convinced of their ability to read their professors' minds, Mr. Martin. To find you included in that group is not particularly reassuring.

As you can see, STUDENT hasn't a prayer. Nothing that he can say will do anything but provide the professor with additional opportunities to humiliate him. Mr. Martin has conceded, without even a struggle, that he doesn't really care anything about passing the course, and is busily engaged in proving that with every word that comes out of his mouth. He should extricate himself from this somehow, but doing it gracefully would be a major project, and we won't take it up at this time. Just thanking DR. LOPEZ for his time and fleeing will suffice for the moment.

There are two ways to respond to a Section F attack without being trampled into the earth like the unfortunate Mr. Martin. The first is one of those memorizable-for-emergency-use sequences, and it goes like this:

"That seems perfectly reasonable."

Think about this now. Someone has said to you that a person who really wanted to pass the course would do certain things. When you reply with "That seems perfectly reasonable," what have you accomplished?

Provided you have done this right, with neutral voice and expression, and in full Computer Mode, you have flatly denied that you are the "a person" being referred to. Since a Section F depends on the attacker being able to maintain the position that he or she has never claimed that you *were* that person, this goes a long way toward defusing the situation. Secondly, you, like your opponent, have made no reference whatsoever to your paper, your research, or your typing. Furthermore, you have—on the surface—agreed with every word being said to you. The professor now has only two choices. He can switch to a much less impressive technique and accuse you outright, like this:

> "Then will you please explain to me why your paper is abominably researched and looks as if it had been typed by a chimpanzee?"

Or alternatively, he can move to a continuing abstract discussion of research and typing of papers by persons unknown and carry that on at any length he wishes, always in Computer Mode. And STUDENT should do precisely the same thing until escape becomes possible or desirable.

All of which brings us to an interesting point.

There are exceptions, of course, depending upon skill and context and many other real-world factors. But as a basic rule of thumb, we can say that except for Levelers, any confrontation between two individuals using the same Satir Mode will not go anywhere useful. More individuals added to the group, also using the same Satir Mode, will make the results no more productive. The fact that most individuals on committees carry on the entire meeting in Computer Mode is probably the major reason why anything accomplished by a committee takes so long and is so minor in relation to the amount of energy and resources poured into the undertaking.

Placating at a Placater is an endless waste of time; Blaming at a Blamer always means a shouting match that degenerates into total futility; Distracting at a Distractor is an interaction between two chaoses, and the result cannot even be referred to as communication. Two Computers talking to one another *sound* better—and in fact, often sound as if something significant were taking place—

but very little actually happens. One of the priceless survival skills in the academic world (and elsewhere, I suspect) is the ability to utter sequences in Computer Mode, within the field of discussion, for almost any length of time and at a moment's notice, without ever saying *anything* with significant content. For example:

> "There appears to be a significant probability, provided all parameters are maximized to their fullest potential within the constraints of demographic variance, that none of the anticipated data will demonstrate behavior atypical of that which one might encounter within the less constrained environment of either the behavioral objectives, so to speak, or the derivationally motivated contingency. This is of course somewhat oversimplified, but its implications need not be belabored, since they will be obvious to all of you, and you need only refer to the relevant literature (which, I might add, is abundant) for further details."

I put that together myself; I can go on like that without a pause for hours at a time if need be. And so far as I myself can determine, if the sequence has any meaning at all it is entirely accidental. If I face an academic group and go through that sequence with a straight face, behaving as if I thought it meant something, I can be quite confident of the response. People will take notes (the content of which I cannot imagine), and they will nod wisely to indicate their agreement; and it will be a rare and star-studded occasion for me when someone raises a hand and says, "You know, I do not have the faintest idea what that means—if anything."

Learn a few paragraphs like the example above. If you cannot construct them yourself, look through half a dozen scholarly journals, or the journals of your trade, until you have collected at least three; then memorize them for future use. I am deadly serious about this. So long as they are sufficiently empty of content, you will be able to use them in any confrontation with someone else using Computer Mode, and they will serve to fill up time while you plan your next move.

Is there an appropriate response to a paragraph like mine, if you find yourself obligated to respond and don't want to bother with another paragraph just like it? Yes, indeed. Look calm, raise your eyebrows ever so slightly, nod a very limited nod that indicates how polite you are, and say, "Except, of course, in the New Hebrides." (Whatever follows "Except, of course" may be any time or place or situation or entirely fictitious study or anything else you care to put there.) "Except, of course, if one must allow for the metric system." "Except, of course, in the work of Gableframe-Socioalwitz." "Except, of course, in the latter part of the rainy season." It makes no difference at all and will have one of two effects. To those who know that the original utterance was a put-on, it will be clear that you know that, too; and you will earn a status point and slide up the pecking order a bit as someone who has to be watched out for. To those who have no idea that the original bit was anything but scholarly and profound, or evidence of expert knowledge, *you* will appear to be scholarly and profound, or expert. Neither outcome can do you any harm.

The jargon of the communication area you are functioning in must be acquired at once. Whether it is political science, bartending, military strategy, professional football, retail sales, housewifery, surgery, or any of the multitude of other possibilities makes no difference. Learn the jargon, commit the list of essential words and phrases (meaningless or not) to memory, and begin using them with your peers. They are as crucial to your verbal self-defense as your hands and feet would be if you were learning karate; without them you are marked, *automatically,* as a victim.

Way back at the beginning of this chapter I told you there were two possible ways to respond to a Section F attack. We have discussed the first at great length. I would now like to move on to the other and then close the chapter with your two practice confrontations.

Look at the following:

X: A person who has serious emotional problems cannot possibly be expected to deal with the constant pressure and tension in this particular department.

Y: I couldn't agree with you more. The problem is, of course, deciding how a situation of this kind should be dealt with.

Y's response, like the "That seems perfectly reasonable" one, appears to be full agreement with the attacker and denies that the speaker is the unknown "A person" under attack. But it raises the level of play by introducing a presupposition that not only are the two of you in agreement, but you have in mind a particular person—not yourself—about whom the *two* of you agree that he or she has serious emotional problems, and so on. This is going to be awkward for your opponent, since you provide no way of determining who that person is and to ask you would look very foolish. Let's see how that might go.

CONFRONTATION FOURTEEN

Employer: A person who has serious emotional problems cannot possibly be expected to deal with the constant pressure and tension in this particular department.

Employee: I couldn't agree with you more. The problem is, of course, deciding how a situation of this kind should be dealt with.

Employer: [Lengthy silence.]

Employee: You're quite right. There are no solutions that leap to the tip of one's tongue.

Employer: Well . . . Miss Wong . . . what do *you* think ought to be the first step? [This is called fishing.]

Employee: Frankly, it's entirely outside my own area of expertise. That you called me in on the matter is gratifying, but I'm afraid that you overestimate the scope of my competence.

Employer: I see. Well, thank you, Miss Wong.

Employee: Not at all. It's unfortunate that I've no really useful input to offer, but I'm quite sure you'll find someone on the staff—or perhaps an outside expert—who will be able to clear things up satisfactorily.

This is an impressive performance on Miss Wong's part. She has left EMPLOYER, who called her in to use a little verbal battery about her alleged "serious emotional problems," in a state of some confusion. EMPLOYER must now find out if some genuinely grave situation exists in the department about which Miss Wong—and perhaps "everyone" except himself—knows. This should distract him from Miss Wong's hypothetical deficiencies for some time. And it is not difficult to carry off a defense of this kind, I assure you. Just practice.

Now here are your practice sets:

CONFRONTATION FIFTEEN

Salesperson: A person who really takes the safety of his family seriously would never buy one of those compact sedans, sir—I tell you that from long experience.

Customer: ______________________________

____

____

Salesperson: ____

____

____

Customer: ____

____

____

(Who won?)

CONFRONTATION SIXTEEN

(Note: It's very common for the neutral "A person who" to be some more precise term in context such as "A woman who" or "A minister who" and so on. This narrows the territory, but does not change the strategy.)

State Policeman: A driver who has any concern for the lives and safety of other people on the road would never change lanes the way you just did, my friend.

Driver: ____

____

____

State Policeman: ____

____

A Person Who . . .

____

Driver: ______________________________

____

____

(Who won?)

YOUR JOURNAL
SECTION F ATTACKS ON ME:

(1) Date ______________________________

Situation ______________________________

____

FIRST MOVE - What My Opponent Said ______________

____

____

What I Said ______________________________

____

____

What I Should Have Said ______________________

____

____

SECOND MOVE - What My Opponent Said ___________

____

____

What I Said ______________________________

____

____

What I Should Have Said ______________________

____

THIRD MOVE - What My Opponent Said ___________

What I Said ___________

What I Should Have Said ___________

FOURTH MOVE - What My Opponent Said ___________

What I Said ___________

What I Should Have Said ___________

---

(2) Date ___________

Situation ___________

FIRST MOVE - What My Opponent Said ____________

____

____

What I Said ______________________________

____

____

What I Should Have Said ___________________

____

____

SECOND MOVE - What My Opponent Said _________

____

____

What I Said ______________________________

____

____

What I Should Have Said ___________________

____

____

THIRD MOVE - What My Opponent Said __________

____

____

What I Said ______________________________

____

____

What I Should Have Said ______________________

____

____

FOURTH MOVE - What My Opponent Said __________

____

____

What I Said _________________________________

____

____

What I Should Have Said ______________________

____

____

SAMPLE SCRIPTS

CONFRONTATION FIFTEEN

Salesperson: A person who really takes the safety of his family seriously would never buy one of those compact sedans, sir—I tell you that from long experience.

Customer: That seems perfectly reasonable.

Salesperson: Then you'll be wanting one of our *larger* models.

Customer: No, I want one of the little ones, thanks.

CUSTOMER wins. For SALESPERSON to attempt to make

CUSTOMER feel guilty, by insinuating that he doesn't care if his family goes to a bloody or fiery death on the highway, is contemptible. It's none of SALESPERSON's business how you feel about your family's safety, unless you've asked for advice on this matter. SALESPERSON will be feeling either confused or foolish at this point, and that's fine.

Salesperson: A person who really takes the safety of his family seriously would never buy one of those compact sedans, sir—I tell you that from long experience.

Customer: I couldn't agree with you more. The problem, of course, is deciding whether to blame the automobile manufacturers, the government, or the advertising agencies.

Salesperson: Well, the *point* is that those little cars are death traps.

Customer: The studies on the question of responsibility just don't get to the heart of the problem, as you are of course aware.

Pretty soon, SALESPERSON should catch on to the fact that CUSTOMER is not going to play this game and will switch to some other strategy. CUSTOMER is winning.

Salesperson: A person who really takes the safety of his family seriously would never buy one of those compact sedans, sir—I tell you that from long experience.

Customer: That seems perfectly reasonable to me. What doesn't seem reasonable is that—given your long experience—you're willing to sell those little death traps.

Salesperson: Now, look, I only *work* here. I don't order the merchandise.

Customer: I see. Well, that must pose a serious ethical problem for you, since you have to sell a product you consider unsafe. How do you handle that?

Game, set, and match to CUSTOMER. What is surprising here is SALESPERSON's lack of skill. Salespeople, especially professional full-time salesmen of expensive items such as automobiles, are ordinarily far better trained in verbal interaction than the average person. SALESPERSON'S response was an amateurish mistake, and if the boss has heard it, SALESPERSON is going to be on the carpet trying to explain how this particular trip down the garden path came about. SALESPERSON should have known better than to take CUSTOMER'S bait.

Salesperson: A person who really takes the safety of his family seriously would never buy one of those compact sedans, sir—I tell you that from long experience.

Customer: You really mean that? I *care* about my family. I don't intend to take any chances, if you know what I mean.

Salesperson: I tell you . . . the company has to provide what the public wants, and a lot of the public wants compact cars. But I wouldn't risk my family in one, and I'm glad to see that you're the sort of person who has better sense than to just go along with the herd.

Customer: Well . . . it's a lot of money, and I was hoping for something with better mileage. But if it's a matter of *safety,* that's got to come first.

SALESPERSON has won, and CUSTOMER hasn't even put up a mild struggle here. Notice, too, that in SALESPER-

SON's second move the responsibility for the product claimed to be unsafe has been adroitly dumped on the unthinking public. This is what SALESPERSON is *supposed* to do, by contrast with the previous example.

CONFRONTATION SIXTEEN

State Policeman: A driver who has any concern for the lives and safety of other people on the road would never change lanes the way you just did, my friend.

Driver: That seems perfectly reasonable.

State Policeman: Then why did you do it?

Driver: I'm sorry, officer, I don't know—and I don't intend to do it again.

Like DOCTOR-PATIENT confrontations, those between officials of the law and alleged breakers of the law are slightly different from the ordinary. DRIVER does not necessarily want to win this one; on the other hand, it isn't necessary to be slavish about it. The example seems to me to have the proper degree of respect for the officer and no more than that.

State Policeman: A driver who has any concern for the lives and safety of other people on the road would never change lanes the way you just did, my friend.

Driver: What makes you think I don't have any concern for other people's safety, officer?

State Policeman: I don't believe this. What makes me think so? I *told* you—that lane change you just made!

Driver: Oh, yeah.

STATE POLICEMAN is right, he did tell you exactly why he thought you were a sadist bent on running down everybody else on the road. This is no time to ask him to repeat it, even if you don't agree with the man's judgment of your lane change.

State Policeman: A driver who has any concern for the lives and safety of other people on the road would never change lanes the way you just did, my friend.

Driver: You're absolutely right. The problem is, of course, what to do in a situation like that.

State Policeman: A situation like what?

Driver: Well, you have a truck bearing down on your bumper from behind, and another truck right in front of you going thirty-five up a hill, and neither of them seems to know you're there. It's a little hard to know what to do in a case like that.

DRIVER is doing fine here; and provided that he or she really was in a situation where an otherwise dangerous lane change seemed to be the only choice available, this is a good way to approach the discussion. DRIVER has begun by agreeing with STATE POLICEMAN and has not offered an excuse for the lane change until asked for it. This racks up a few points in DRIVER's favor. Furthermore, DRIVER has managed to shift the discussion from this specific lane change toward the question of lane change strategies in general. Well done.

State Policeman: A driver who has any concern for the lives and safety of other people on the road would never change lanes the way you just did, my friend.

Driver: You may be right, but let me tell *you*, officer, I was really in a bind back there. I notice you saw me make a lane change . . . how about the guy that was running me off the damned *road?* How come you aren't stopping *him?*

State Policeman: My, you're a polite one, aren't you? You have anything else to tell me about how I ought to do my job?

Driver: Yeah, as a matter of fact I do. My taxes pay your salary, you know.

I assume no comment is needed here. If you are looking for a strategy to use in confrontations with policemen that will guarantee you an expensive ticket, talking to them in Blamer Mode like this is certainly it. DRIVER cannot possibly win.

Section G Attacks

Why Don't You Ever . . .

10

You will immediately recognize the Section G pattern as an attack in Blamer Mode and one that can be flipped tidily on its back to a "Why do you always . . . " form. (Flipped like that, of course, the attack becomes so nearly identical to its presupposition—that you "always" do whatever is stated—that the difference between them isn't worth mentioning.) The basic form is this:

> "Why don't you ever (X)?"

Almost anything can be fit into the empty (X) term of the pattern. For example:

"Why don't you ever
- try to make me happy?"
- consider anybody's feelings but your own?"
- act like other people's mothers?"
- do anything that *I* would enjoy doing?"
- want anybody else to have any fun?"
- think about the effect of your behavior on the other people in this class?"

"Why do you always
- get such a kick out of seeing me miserable?"
- try to make me look like an idiot?"
- knock yourself out to ruin things for everybody else?"
- deliberately embarrass me in every way you can?"
- spoil anything good that happens to come along for anybody else?"

The presupposition of "Why don't you ever (X)?" that is relevant for verbal self-defense is simply "You never (X)." It is certainly neither subtle nor intricate. Why, then, have I put it all the way up at the G level in difficulty instead of letting it share bottom rank with "If you *really* . . . "? Obviously it is not here because it presents levels of interacting and well-hidden presuppositions that require great skill to disentangle. The problems with the Section G attack are the following:

1. Most of them come at you from people who, because you are involved in a close relationship with them, have a real power to cause you pain. Unlike the teacher you see for only one semester of an academic year or the mechanic that you take your car to only once, people who hit you with Section G's tend to be people you spend large portions of your life with. You can't say to yourself, "Oh, well, it's only sixteen weeks and then I'll never have to go near this person for the rest of my life." Because Section G's have their source in people you must interact with closely and constantly, they are unusually difficult to manage.

2. Leading right from the first problem is the fact that people in a position to try a Section G on you usually know your most vulnerable spots. If you worry because you think you're too thin or because you didn't finish high school or right on up the scale to such problems as alcoholism or bankruptcy, these people probably know about that. They may have been around you most of your life, and as a result they know *exactly* where to put the knife and how many twists of it are required to get to you.
3. Because the Section G's are so personal, and so vicious, they face you with a tremendous temptation to respond by

Your Personal Octagon

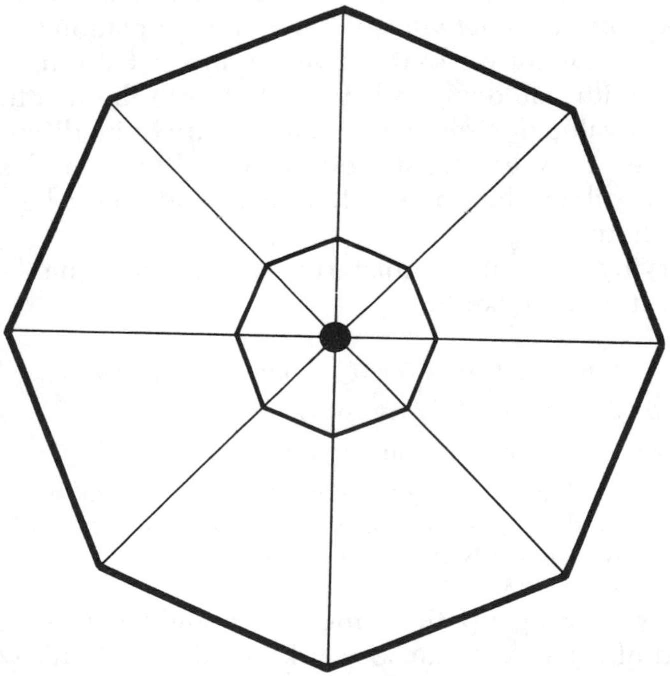

> hurting back. That is, you are likely to know as much about your attacker's weak spots as he or she does about yours. And in a sort of blind reaction to pain you tend to go straight to Blamer Mode yourself and head straight into a full-scale disaster, full of things that can never really be forgotten, even though they may be forgiven. Furthermore, if you have become highly skilled at verbal self-defense, you may be able to do harm for which you will never be able to forgive yourself.

These three factors, taken together, seem to me to cause a Section G to merit the next-to-last spot in the ranking of difficulty. (And I may have underestimated; perhaps they should be at the very top.)

If you value the relationship you have with a Section G opponent, you *must not* give in to the temptation to hurt back. That cannot work; it is two primitives battering one another with boulders, and it is a battle to the death. (If you don't value the relationship, things are quite different, of course, and your best strategy is probably just to leave. That's a subject for some other book and won't be discussed here.)

Trying to argue against the accusation won't help, either. It will go like this:

X: Why don't you ever try to make me happy?
You: Sweetheart, I *do* try to make you happy!
X: When? Just tell me *one time* you did that!
You: Well, don't you remember the time that [and here you produce your example, or list of examples, and you will feel silly doing it].

If you bring up the time you bought a Chevrolet instead of a Jaguar because you knew that X didn't want a Jaguar, you'll hear that the only reason you did that was because the Chevrolet was cheaper and furthermore you've never stopped rubbing X's nose in that one. If you bring up the time you gave up a trip to San Francisco at company expense because X couldn't go and didn't want you to go on that basis, you'll hear that the real reason you did that was to have the satisfaction of telling everybody how narrow-minded X is and hearing them laugh about it. It won't get better—it will go on like that. For every token you offer, every shred of proof that you have tried to make X happy, X will have an alternative explanation that fits the picture of the world in which all your energies are devoted to making him or her miserable. As your shreds of proof grow more trivial, you will feel more and more ridiculous. And you should. You should never start one of these absurd lists; that went out with gallant knights bringing fair maidens one token after another to be rejected contemptuously. "Remember the time I went out and killed nine giants at a blow and brought you back their heads?" This *is* ridiculous, and stupid. Don't do it.

The only effective nonviolent response to a Section G is one in which you do the following: *Immediately say something which, in itself, disproves the claim your attacker is making.* Preferably by offering something you know quite well that he or she doesn't want at all. For example:

Husband: Why don't you ever try to make me happy?

Wife: Sweetheart, do you think maybe you'd be happier if we both quit our jobs and moved to Wyoming? [Be certain before you do this that he does *not* want either of you to quit your jobs or move to Wyoming—or be prepared to follow through and keep your mouth shut about it.]

The sequence looks simpleminded; I agree. But the attack itself is simpleminded, and it deserves a simpleminded response, not a subtle one. HUSBAND has claimed that WIFE never—not ever, not even once—does anything to try to make him happy. Immediately, without a second's delay, she proves him wrong; her response is an attempt to make him happy. It is an act as well as an utterance, and it falsifies his claim on the spot.

The fact that it is outrageous has no relevance here. In fact, it may well be that the more outrageous it is—so long as it does not make HUSBAND feel he is being made fun of—the better it is. Especially if he intensely does not want to accept whatever is being offered in an attempt to "make him happy," it should cause him to drop the attack and devote his energies to heading off the offer. Above all, it will head off the list of proofs from the past, each of which he intended to painstakingly expose as not a genuine attempt to make him happy. This is what matters most of all. Let's try carrying this out for a few moves.

CONFRONTATION SEVENTEEN

Husband: Why don't you ever try to make me happy?

Wife: Sweetheart, do you think maybe you'd be happier if we both quit our jobs and moved to Wyoming?

Husband: [Stunned silence.]

Wife: Honey? Would you like that?

Husband: The last thing on this *earth* I would ever want to see happen is both of us quitting our jobs and moving to Wyoming!

Wife: Well, then, let's not. I'm perfectly content with the way things are.

Husband: Move to Wyoming . . . pheew."

Wife: Since that's settled, what would you like to do for dinner tonight?

If this happens every time HUSBAND tries a Section

G, he will give them up. They're no fun at all if the other person involved won't play the game. They're rewarding only if they allow a long wallow in past regrets, broken promises, inadequate compromises, and all the rest of it. If they are instantly refuted with an offer like the one in Confrontation Seventeen, it will become clear to HUSBAND—although it may take a while—that this technique is never going to pay off.

Section G's should be looked upon as a bad habit to be broken, like spitting in public. They should be a habit you can break the other person of just this simply, and reasonably quickly, by taking all the fun out of them. If you can't—if HUSBAND, or whoever the other individual may be, persists in spite of your efforts over several months—then you don't need verbal self-defense. You need an expert to find out what's wrong. That goes far beyond the scope of this book.

Once in a while a Section G will come your way from someone who is not particularly close to you and doesn't fit the typical pattern. You may just happen to have a boss who is a natural bully and enjoys the Blamer role. Unless you let this get to you and make you miserable, it's trivial; and it can be handled in exactly the same way as the more classic situation. For example:

CONFRONTATION EIGHTEEN

Employer: Why don't you ever, even once, consider the feelings of the other people in this office and try to do something that would make life pleasanter for *them* instead of thinking only of yourself?

Employee: Okay . . . how about if all the coffee breaks were thirty minutes instead of fifteen. I think that might do it.

Employer: Thirty-minute coffee breaks? You're out of your

mind! We'd never get any work done around here.

Employee: Well, you're the boss.

Like I said, this is trivial. Just be sure to pick something that the boss would never under any circumstances consider doing, but which will stand, in itself, as a refutation of the accusation. The principle is the same as in Confrontation Seventeen, but the stakes are lower.

Now here are your practice confrontations, with sample scripts at the end of the chapter.

CONFRONTATION NINETEEN

Daughter: Why do you always have to be different? Why can't you ever be like other mothers, anyway?

Mother: ____

____

____

Daughter: ____

____

____

Mother: ____

____

____

Daughter: ____

____

____

Mother: ____

____

____

(Who won?)

CONFRONTATION TWENTY

Woman: Why do you always go out of your way to make me look stupid and ignorant in front of all your friends? Why don't you ever let me have a chance to show people that *I* know something, too?

Man: ____

____

____

Woman: ____

____

____

Man: ____

____

____

Woman: ____

____

____

Man: ____

____

____

(Who won?)

YOUR JOURNAL
SECTION G ATTACKS ON ME:

(1) Date ____________________

Situation ____________________

____

FIRST MOVE - What My Opponent Said ____________________

____

____

What I Said ____________________

____

____

What I Should Have Said ____________________

____

____

SECOND MOVE - What My Opponent Said ____________________

____

____

What I Said ____________________

____

____

What I Should Have Said ____________________

____

____

THIRD MOVE - What My Opponent Said ____________

____

____

What I Said ______________________________

____

____

What I Should Have Said ________________

____

____

FOURTH MOVE - What My Opponent Said __________

____

____

What I Said ______________________________

____

____

What I Should Have Said ________________

____

____

(2) Date ______________________________________

Situation ________________________________

____

FIRST MOVE - What My Opponent Said ____________

____

____

What I Said ________________________________

____

____

What I Should Have Said ____________________

____

____

SECOND MOVE - What My Opponent Said _________

____

____

What I Said ________________________________

____

____

What I Should Have Said ____________________

____

____

THIRD MOVE - What My Opponent Said __________

____

____

What I Said ________________________________

____

____

What I Should Have Said ______________________________

____

____

FOURTH MOVE - What My Opponent Said ______________________________

____

____

What I Said ______________________________

____

____

What I Should Have Said ______________________________

____

____

SAMPLE SCRIPTS

CONFRONTATION NINETEEN

Daughter: Why do you always have to be different? Why can't you ever be like other mothers, anyway?

Mother: Okay. From now on, like other mothers, I'm giving you a ten o'clock curfew on school nights.

Daughter: But, Mother—

Mother: And, like other mothers, I'll expect you to be in by eleven on Saturday night. Does that solve your problem?

Daughter: That's not fair!

Mother: Really? Let me introduce you, my dear, to the

real world, in which *many* things are not fair. Including lots of other people's mothers.

If you wrote something like this, it's hard to know where you're headed without also knowing the teen-age DAUGHTER you had in mind. True, this move on MOTHER'S part immediately negates the claim that MOTHER is never like other mothers and does it by offering something MOTHER can be certain DAUGHTER doesn't want. This is fully in accord with the instructions for responding to a Section G, and it may have been called for, depending on the DAUGHTER in question. However, there's no winner here; it's a standoff. DAUGHTER feels resentful, and if in fact she didn't deserve this, she has been smacked down as surely as if MOTHER had used an open hand; and she won't forget it. The injury will fester. MOTHER feels smug right now, especially after the very "grown-up" finish line, but will probably feel ashamed of herself later. What MOTHER has accomplished in this example is the teaching of a lesson: Do not try being a Blamer at me because I am bigger and more powerful than you and I will see to it that you regret it. This may be temporarily satisfying, but it has two certain effects: (a) to reinforce DAUGHTER in the Blamer pattern; and (b) to ensure total noncommunication with DAUGHTER, who'll go do her Blaming on someone her own size in the future.

Daughter: Why do you always have to be different? Why can't you ever be like other mothers, anyway?

Mother: Well, let's see. Would I seem more like other mothers to you, honey, if I always waited up for you when you go out at night? And then you could come sit on my bed, and we could have a nice cozy chat about what your evening was like, and what everybody was wearing . . . you know, girl talk. Would you like that?

Daughter: Good grief. That would be horrible.

Mother: Well, then, we certainly don't have to do it.

Much better, and no further moves needed. If the custom described above is already observed in this household, and enjoyed by both MOTHER and DAUGHTER, it's not an option (though something else can be used in its place). But most American teen-age daughters do not want this ritual added to their lives. On the other hand, it fits superbly into the traditional image of the Devoted, Caring Mother Like Other Mothers and is an instant offer—which the Blaming DAUGHTER must turn down. MOTHER wins, without turning into a heavy parent figure, and without much effort.

MOTHER must be careful not to overdo this, however, or DAUGHTER will think she is being made fun of. If "nice cozy chat" won't get by this DAUGHTER, MOTHER can pare it back to "a discussion of your evening." It must be played absolutely straight.

Daughter: Why do you always have to be different? Why can't you ever be like other mothers, anyway?

Mother: I'm different from other mothers? Hmmm. How about if I cut my hair and quit wearing these jeans?

Daughter: That wasn't the kind of thing I meant.

Mother: You don't want me to look like other mothers?

Daughter: No! I like the way you look.

Mother: Well, then, I don't know—you want to talk about it awhile?

As with the move to Wyoming, MOTHER should be sure that the offer she makes is either something she doesn't mind doing or that DAUGHTER will be certain to refuse. Assuming that this is true, she has done well and is winning. MOTHER has refused the "you never" presupposition, since lots of mothers don't wear jeans and do cut their hair. She has done it immediately, with no Blaming involved. And she has now a potential here now for some productive Leveling.

Daughter: Why do you always have to be different? Why can't you ever be like other mothers, anyway?

Mother: Because you don't act like other *daughters*, that's why. And until you do, I don't intend to put myself out for you.

Daughter: Thanks a lot, Mother. I'll try to keep that in mind.

Mother: You do that. And if you find yourself forgetting it, try another smart crack and I'll help you remember.

Daughter: Thanks—I won't need any help.

Mother: You're quite welcome. Drop in and have a little chat *any*time.

Very, very bad. Here we have two Blamers, whacking away at each other with fang and claw. MOTHER is serving superbly as a role model in this example, training DAUGHTER in all the finer nuances of being an adult Blamer. She'll regret it eventually—and nobody wins.

CONFRONTATION TWENTY

Woman: Why do you always go out of your way to make me look stupid and ignorant in front of all your friends? Why don't you ever let me have a chance to show people that *I* know something, too?

Man: Okay, sweetheart. Next time the subject of oil depletion allowances comes up, you handle it.

Woman: You're *still* doing it!

Man: Doing what?

Woman: You know perfectly well what!

Man: Sorry—you've lost me.

MAN appears to be a chronic verbal abuser, if this is any sample of his behavior, and WOMAN is getting nowhere with the problem of defending herself. He has responded with an immediate offer to show people that she, too, can shine in conversation and has carefully chosen something that he knows she doesn't want. But he has also carefully chosen something he knows quite well she knows nothing about, something that she would look stupid and ignorant discussing, and by so doing has (as she points out) demonstrated to her once again how stupid and ignorant she is. (Laying herself open to this kind of thing *is* stupid and ignorant, by the way.) She then goes right on Blaming, and MAN enjoys himself at her expense. Total silence would be less of a waste of time.

Woman: Why do you always go out of your way to make me look stupid and ignorant in front of all your friends? Why don't you ever let me have a chance to show people that *I* know something, too?

Man: Okay, sweetheart. How about if we give a big party—I mean a *really* big party—and we ask everybody we usually see around and whoever else you'd like to ask. And I promise to keep my big mouth *shut* and let you do the talking.

Woman: Oh, dear . . .

Man: Something wrong? Look, I wouldn't mind doing that at all.

Woman: I hate parties. Especially big parties.

Man: Then we don't have to do it. It was just an idea.

Very well done. MAN needs to demonstrate to WOMAN that the Section G is not a productive way to talk about things, and he's done that. At the same time he's made her an offer of exactly what she appeared to be asking for, choosing something he could be sure she wouldn't care to accept. And of course he closes by reassuring her that he's not about to insist on her doing something she'd rather not do. It will take considerable ingenuity on WOMAN's part to find anything to complain about here.

Woman: Why do you always go out of your way to make me look stupid and ignorant in front of all your friends? Why don't you ever let me have a chance to show people that *I* know something, too?

Man: Because, my sweet, you are unable to hold up your end of a conversation on any subject except dieting and toilet training.

Woman: Your friends could use some current information on both topics.

Man: You know what you deserve? You deserve for me to *let* you make a fool of yourself!

Woman: Does it make you feel important to talk to me like that? Do you enjoy that?

Man: [Sigh] If you *really* wanted to look intelligent, darling, you'd make an effort to learn something worth talking about.

The only difference between this WOMAN's behavior and that of the one in the first example in this confrontation is that she has learned to do her Blaming with a bit more sophistication. The only result is that MAN will return the ball with more force. Notice that he is now headed full-swing into a different attack and is moving into more and more violent Blamer Mode with each move. This one is hopeless—and WOMAN will lose.

Woman: Why do you always go out of your way to make me look stupid and ignorant in front of all your friends? Why don't you ever let me have a chance to show people that *I* know something, too?

Man: You know, if I'm doing that, I should be ashamed of myself. Tell you what. You pick out a list of things you'd like to talk about next time we go out, and I'll promise to stay clear away from every one of them. Fair enough?

Woman: No! Then I'd really look silly!

Man: Why? Isn't that what you wanted?

Woman: No! That's not what I meant at all. It would be obvious . . . and artificial . . . and . . .

Man: Well, look, you want to stop someplace for coffee and talk about this? I don't seem to be getting the message.

This is well handled. The first offer MAN makes is sufficiently strange to be unlikely of acceptance, but it qualifies as doing what WOMAN says he never does. And it doesn't humiliate her or blame her, so long as he is careful to keep a neutral stance and sound perfectly serious. If WOMAN takes him up on the offer to talk this over, they may be able to do some Leveling and accomplish something. If she doesn't, he has at least headed off the argument, and there will be other chances to discuss the problem.

MAN is the winner, nonviolently, and is definitely not encouraging WOMAN in this particular pattern for working out their difficulties. That's the primary goal, and he's following through properly.

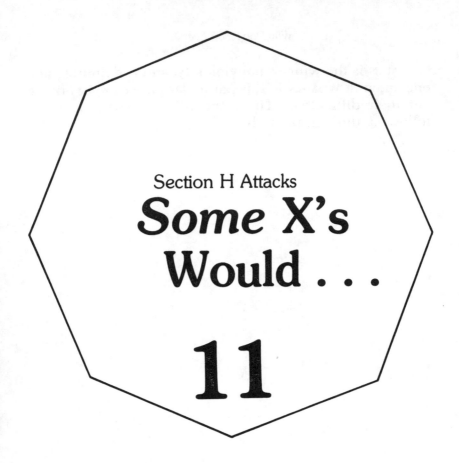

Section H Attacks

Some X's Would . . .

11

We are now at the last of the attacks on the Octagon—Section H. Its basic pattern looks like this:

> "*Some* (X's) would (Y) if/when (Z) (W)."

We have a lot of unfilled terms there, each with its own potential for trouble. Because of the possibility for confusion as we take up the empty pieces one at a time, a sample with everything filled in would be a good way to begin. For instance:

> "*Some* instructors would really become angry when a student handed in a paper that looked like this one."

If we label the parts in that example to match the pattern in the box, the breakdown looks like this:

> "*Some* instructors [X's] would really become angry [Y] when a student [Z] handed in a paper that looked like this one [W]."

The heavy stress on the word "Some" at the beginning is important. As is often the case with emphatic stress, removing it changes the meaning of the sequence—which means that the presuppositions are different. Without the heavy stress the sequence is not a Section H, but a neutral statement of opinion; thus, the stress is crucial.

Possible ways to fill in each of the empty terms should now be more easy to follow. We'll go straight down the line.

"*Some* (X) husbands
bosses
kids
patients
people
lawyers
would (Y) really not be able to understand
resent it very much
really get mad
be absolutely shocked
not stand for it for one minute
when/if (Z) you
a student
a customer

Your Personal Octagon

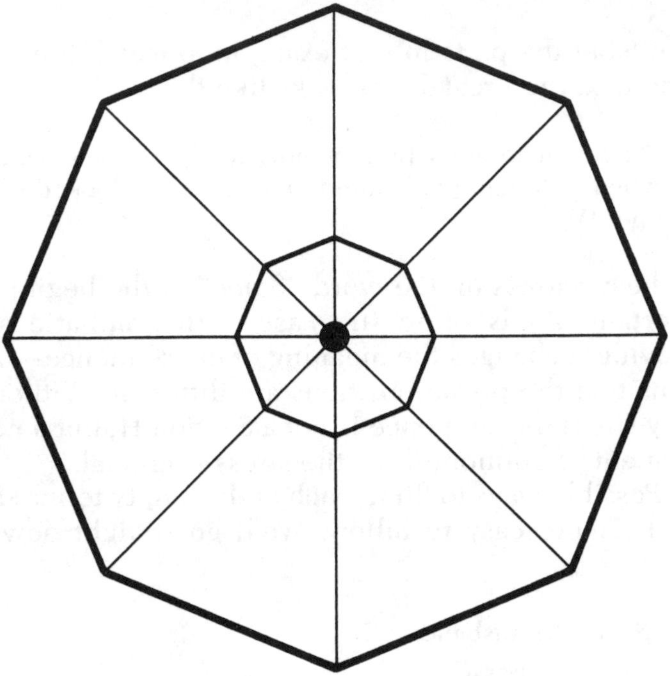

© Suzette Haden Elgin 1978

somebody who ought to know better

a full-grown woman

(W) always comes to class late with a ridiculous excuse."
lost her job for the second time in one year."
never had time to talk to them for more than three minutes and then charged them $25."

(X) can be any set of individuals which the speaker considers himself or herself to be a member of. (Z) may be filled by anything at all that the speaker cares to use to represent the person spoken *to*—and it may very well contain within it other moves from the Octagon. For example, (Z) may turn up as "a person who doesn't even *care* about the effect her smoking has on other people around her." Or worse.

Deep water, agreed? However, despite the pileup of possibilities here, and the potential for intricate presuppositions nested inside other presuppositions, there is nothing *new*. It is just a matter of carefully taking the big pieces apart into smaller pieces and proceeding with each of them separately. The difficulty in the real world is, of course, that you have to do this in your head, do it very fast, and not get mixed up. I suggest lots of practice, and plenty of work in your Journal, unless you find that you can do this with ease. Working your way in writing through a few dozen Section H attacks that are completely hypothetical, so that you can spend all the time you like thinking them through, will pay off the first time you find yourself facing a real one with about five seconds lead time.

If we return to the first example sentence in this chapter—"*Some* instructors would really become angry when a student handed in a paper that looked like this one"—we can list its relevant presuppositions as follows:

1. "Your paper is an absolute mess, a disgrace, an object that no ordinary instructor would even consider accepting."
2. "I'm not *like* other instructors; I'm unique, and quite superior to them."
3. "The reason that I am unique and superior is that I am going to accept your paper."
4. "You should feel very, very guilty and ashamed about your paper."
5. "You should feel very, very grateful to *me*, your unique and superior instructor."

Yes, Virginia, all of that most assuredly is in there. And often there's a good deal more, depending on the particular situation; for instance, there may be a presupposition that the speaker has the authority and power to let you do something or keep you from doing it.

A Section H attack is in Computer Mode throughout, if it is well done. If the person using it fills term (Z) with the word "you"—as in "*Some* guys would really get mad if you . . . ," that is an indication of little or no skill. The bait is whatever turns up in (W), and it should be ignored, like the bait in any other attack. If you fall for the bait, YOU WILL LOSE. Period. You cannot take it and win, no matter how great it makes you feel to surge into battle against this inexcusable accusation and shout your outrage and so on. You may enjoy that for a few minutes, but you will lose.

I have two suggestions for your response to a Section H. The first is more personal than the second; both are quite gentle; and either will do the job. Your choice depends on how pleasant you care to be to this person. Remember your basic pattern: "*Some* persons [identified by your opponent] would react in a particular way to what you are [claimed to be] doing." That's what you will hear. And you should respond like this:

> "Really? It would be interesting to hear *your* opinion on the matter, darling [or "Mr. White" or "Dr. Blue," or whatever is appropriate]."

This a skilled move. First of all, it blandly denies the most crucial of the presuppositions, as in the "A person who . . . " attack. It denies that you are the individual being referred to in (Z). Since your attacker has not said that you *were* that person, he or she has only been agreed with on what you are treating as a neutral abstract statement about opinions or reactions that some people might have. You have not taken the bait. Furthermore, you have complimented your attacker by asking for his or her opinion, even though you know quite well that you have really just heard that opinion given. You now have your Section H person in a tidy bind, and it is you who are winning.

An alternative response, if you don't care much about this person, is the following:

> "That's been said a good deal and is undoubtedly an interesting idea."

Now *wait*, looking very calm and only mildly interested. This is full Computer Mode. It accomplishes the same goal of removing you personally from the confrontation and denying that you are involved. It uses the adjective "interesting" to refer to what's just been said; and in America "interesting" is the adjective you use when you do not wish to commit yourself either for or against something. If a friend asks whether you like the sonata she has just composed, and you despise it, but you either don't feel competent to judge it or don't want to hurt her feelings, you say that it is "interesting." This is the proper move.

There are two reactions that are almost universal in my workshops and training seminars at this point:

> "There's got to be some other way of doing it—that absolutely would not work."

OR . . .

> "I could not *possibly* say either one of those things. No way. Other people, maybe, but I couldn't do it."

But I am obliged to tell you that if you try to make changes in the two responses I've just given you, I can guarantee you the following results: (a) you will change the degree of challenge in your move, either increasing it or decreasing it; (b) you will introduce new presuppositions that you are not likely to have intended and may be entirely unaware of; (c) in all probability, both (a) and (b) will occur.

If you have ever been involved in any of the classical martial arts, you can surely remember a time when the instructor described a move or a stance to you and the situation was analogous to this one. In judo, for example, the instruction to *fall* in a certain way struck me as something I could not believe in and something I could not do.

The responses to Section H are the right ones, they will work, and they should not be monkeyed around with until you are highly skilled. If they sound phony and pretentious to you, that's fine. They are *intended* to do so. The Section H attack is itself phony and pretentious. For you to respond with equal pretentiousness is precisely correct. It will immediately inform your opponent that he or she is not dealing with a naïve victim but with someone who knows just what is going on and is prepared to deal with it. In any martial art there comes a moment when you must trust your instructor, or no progress is possible, and for this one, this is the moment.

There is also a counterattack. Please remember that counterattacks are verbal violence, and that they can rarely be justified. But because the Section H move is so dangerous, and because the person using it is so likely to get you into much thornier thickets than you would anticipate, I feel an obligation to provide it for you. It has an empty spot in it that you will have to fill in, based on your personal knowledge of your opponent; if you have no such knowledge, you'll have to use a neutral sequence and count on the other person to supply it with content. Here you are:

> "I wonder if your mother [or your minister, the public, your supervisor, or your associate] is aware of your position on this matter."

If you use this, *you* have become the attacker. Do it if you must, but only if you must. It's not nice. It will say to your Section H-er that, in your opinion, whoever you have picked out to fill the empty slot probably *doesn't* know about the strange way your attacker is behaving . . . but might well be told, if things go on. It is a threat. The decision to use this is an ethical problem rather than a wholly strategic one.

Let's look at one sample confrontation and then close this chapter with two practice sets for you to work on. The first blank lines you have to fill in should be easy, since you will only have two choices. Going on from there may be more difficult. Here's the sample:

CONFRONTATION TWENTY-ONE

Husband: *Some* husbands would really get upset if their wives insisted on going back to work when the kids were still only babies.

Wife: Really? It would be interesting to hear *your* opinion on the matter, darling.

Husband: *My* opinion is that you have no business going back to work, if you really want to know.

Wife: I see. Well, I'm willing to discuss that idea if you are.

Notice what has happened here. HUSBAND, caught off guard, has abandoned all pretense of being some unique and superior individual to whom WIFE should be grateful in spite of the awful things she is doing; and he has given up Computer Mode for Blamer. Now the issue is right out in the open, and WIFE has made an offer to continue the discussion in Leveler Mode. This is properly done.

CONFRONTATION TWENTY-TWO

Financial Aid Officer: *Some* financial aid officers would be very unlikely to believe a student with a grade point average of only 2.6 and a story like the one that you have just told me, Mr. Everett.

Student: ____

____

____

F. A. O.: ____

____

____

Student: ____

____

____

F. A. O.: ____

____

____

Student: ____

____

____

(Who won?

CONFRONTATION TWENTY-THREE

Mechanic: *Some* skilled mechanics would consider it a real insult if a customer came back and insinuated that work had been done on their car that wasn't really necessary.

Customer: ______________________________

____

____

Mechanic: ______________________________

____

____

Customer: ______________________________

____

____

Mechanic: ______________________________

____

____

Customer: ______________________________

____

____

(Who won?)

YOUR JOURNAL
SECTION H ATTACKS ON ME:

(1) Date ____________________

Situation ____________________

____

FIRST MOVE—What My Opponent Said ____________________

____

____

What I Said ____________________

____

____

What I Should Have Said ____________________

____

____

SECOND MOVE—What My Opponent Said ____________________

____

____

What I Said ____________________

____

____

What I Should Have Said ____________________

____

____

THIRD MOVE—What My Opponent Said __________

____

____

What I Said ______________________________

____

____

What I Should Have Said __________________

____

____

FOURTH MOVE—What My Opponent Said ________

____

____

What I Said ______________________________

____

____

What I Should Have Said __________________

____

____

(2) Date _________________________________

Situation ________________________________

____

FIRST MOVE—What My Opponent Said ____________

____

____

What I Said ______________________________

____

____

What I Should Have Said ____________________

____

____

SECOND MOVE—What My Opponent Said __________

____

____

What I Said ______________________________

____

____

What I Should Have Said ____________________

____

____

THIRD MOVE—What My Opponent Said ____________

____

____

What I Said ______________________________

____

____

What I Should Have Said ____________________

____

____

FOURTH MOVE—What My Opponent Said __________

____

____

What I Said ________________________________

____

____

What I Should Have Said ____________________

____

____

SAMPLE SCRIPTS

CONFRONTATION TWENTY-TWO

Financial Aid Officer: *Some* financial aid officers would be very unlikely to believe a student with a grade point average of only 2.6 and a story like the one you have just told me, Mr. Everett.

Student: Really? It would be interesting to hear *your* opinion on the matter, Mr. Begaye.

F.A.O.: *Dr.* Begaye, Mr. Everett!

Student: Of course, Dr. Begaye. My apologies.

F.A.O.: Now where were we, anyway?

Student: You were about to discuss the attitude of other financial aid officers toward situations of this kind, Dr. Begaye. And I'm looking forward to that—this entire matter is a new area of experience for me.

STUDENT is doing this right—and it isn't easy. Among the other unpalatable facts of life (which I know this book is filled with) is this one: There is no way to ask someone either to loan or to give you money while maintaining an attitude of total independence. *Dignity*, yes; begging is not required. But any person you are asking for money other than at gunpoint is the person in power, and you had better keep that firmly in mind. There's a fine line between respectful attention and bootlicking; you'll need to learn where that line is and how to walk it.

FINANCIAL AIDS OFFICER has given away a few points with his insistence on being called "Dr." rather than "Mr.," which probably means that STUDENT's first move caught him off guard. Only if F.A.O. is insecure in his own estimate of his status would he demand the title in that way. (A Leveler who had to fight hard for a Ph.D. and intends, for any one of a number of good reasons, to have that word "Dr." in front of his or her name, will not make the demand in the form F.A.O. used. Instead, the line will be on the order of "If you don't have any strong objections, I'd rather you called me *Dr.* Begaye.")

By the end of the set of moves in this example, STUDENT has F.A.O. in a position in which it's going to be awkward to return to the original accusation, with all its dangling presuppositions. Who will win is difficult to say, but things are going well. Just remember that if you're asking for money (or any substantial favor), you can't afford to humiliate the person you're asking; on the other hand, money that robs you of all your self-respect is money at too high a price. STUDENT's closing line is just respectful enough.

Financial Aid Officer: *Some* financial aid officers would be very unlikely to believe a student with a grade point average of only 2.6 and a story like the one you have just told me, Mr. Everett.

Student: My story is true. And my grades are as good as anybody's could be with the obligations I have to meet.

F.A.O.: *Mr.* Everett . . . whining is not going to help matters. I sit here all day long and listen to whiners, and I get very tired of it.

Student: Then maybe you're in the wrong job, Mr. Begaye.

F.A.O.: And maybe you are in the wrong *school,* Mr. Everett.

Student: Okay, okay. I get it.

STUDENT gets the message, but not the money; and it took him about three minutes to lose. He now has the satisfaction of his intact pride, but he has no money to pay for his tuition, and he has also given the F.A.O. a chance to dump a lot more abuse on him, for free. This is *not* cost-effective. If STUDENT is going to be turned down for the money anyway, he might at least come out of the verbal confrontation with a few more points earned.

Financial Aid Officer: *Some* financial aid officers would be very unlikely to believe a student with a grade point average of only 2.6 and a story like the one you have just told me, Mr. Everett.

Student: I've heard people say that a lot, and it's an interesting idea.

F.A.O.: You spend a lot of time applying for loans, do you?

Student: Sorry—I don't think I follow you.

F.A.O.: Well, young man, unless your circle of friends includes numerous financial aid officers, bank loan officers, and the like—which I sincerely doubt—I don't know where else you would have heard people discussing the appropriate attitude for officials in charge of disbursements of monies toward dubious applicants.

Student: Sorry. I guess I was out of line.

This is the sort of thing that you risk when you tinker with the response to a Section H. STUDENT's mistake was in not going to Computer Mode—notice that he begins with "I've heard people say that" and leaves himself wide open for F.A.O. to knock around. Which is what happens. The whole point of putting this response into the form "That's been said a good deal," however odd it may sound to you, is to eliminate any overt claim on your part as to who said it or where or when or to whom—and most especially to take you personally out of the sentence. STUDENT's mistake has cost him dearly, whether he gets the loan or not. He ends up Placating and apologizing and generally crawling about on the floor being an animated exercise mat for F.A.O. Not recommended.

Financial Aid Officer: *Some* financial aid officers would be very unlikely to believe a student with a grade point average of only 2.6 and a story like the one you have just told me, Mr. Everett.

Student: One hears that said a good deal. It would be most interesting to hear *your* opinion on the matter, Dr. Begaye.

F.A.O.: One does, does one?

Student: I'm sorry?

F.A.O.: Another thing one hears—if one listens to the right people—is that if you're asking someone for money, you don't start by proving that you could qualify for the Olympic Gold Medal in arrogance.

Student: Yes, sir.

Again, STUDENT has tried to make a few small changes. And it is quite true that the use of the indefinite "one" in his response takes him out of the sentence, puts it in Computer Mode, and is roughly equivalent in meaning to "That's been said a good deal." Unfortunately, by using this construction, STUDENT has escalated the pompousness of the dialogue and outpompoused F.A.O. This is *very* risky. Most people in a position of power, if they have any goodwill in their character, will have reservations about picking on people who aren't remotely their equals in status. But STUDENT has canceled that out. His response says, "Look, you pompous creep, you don't need to use kid gloves on *me*. Anything you can do, I can handle." Once that's done, F.A.O. is no longer bound by any code of not kicking underdogs; on the contrary, STUDENT has specifically released him from that and demanded to be treated as an equal. He has only himself to thank when he gets precisely what he asked for. F.A.O. is playing the game by the rules, right down the line, and STUDENT is going to take a beating, and lose as well.

Be absolutely certain before you declare yourself ready to play verbal games with no holds barred that you really *are* ready. Or that you can afford to look upon being used to mop up a floor as a kind of educational experience.

CONFRONTATION TWENTY-THREE

Mechanic: *Some* skilled mechanics would consider it a real insult if a customer came back and insinuated that work had been done on their car that wasn't really necessary.

Customer: Really? It would be interesting to hear *your* opinion on the matter, Mr. Granger.

Mechanic: You just heard it.

Customer: I don't think I followed you.

Mechanic: You want me to spell it out for you?

Customer: That's an excellent idea.

This is going properly. MECHANIC is now going to have to be absolutely specific, which will give CUSTOMER a chance to deal with the situation on a Leveler basis. And MECHANIC has abandoned his abstract Computer stance without even a struggle. CUSTOMER is way ahead.

Mechanic: *Some* skilled mechanics would consider it a real insult if a customer came back and insinuated that work had been done on their car that wasn't really necessary.

Customer: That's been said a good deal and is undoubtedly an interesting idea.

Mechanic: What do you mean by *that*?

Customer: You read about mechanics who—in spite of their skill—are touchy and defensive about any attempt at a logical, adult discussion of their bills . . . and one can't help wondering why that should be so. After all, the mechanic is the expert, not the customer, right?

Mechanic: Absolutely.

Customer: What do you suppose accounts for this problem, Mr. Granger—speaking as a skilled mechanic yourself?

CUSTOMER is winning, and it will be interesting to see what MECHANIC does next. He can move into an abstract discussion of other mechanics and other estimates, losing money as he whiles away time with this pleasant CUSTOMER who is so interested in all his opinions. Or he can change his strategy and try Leveling. Or he can try to think of something else. He knows of course that CUSTOMER is putting him on, but he started this himself and will have to get out of it the same way.

Mechanic: *Some* skilled mechanics would consider it a real insult if a customer came back and insinuated that work had been done on their car that wasn't really necessary.

Customer: Too bad you aren't a skilled mechanic, then, isn't it?

Mechanic: You want to see my credentials? I'll be only too happy to show them to you. Or perhaps you'd like to speak to the manager of the shop.

Customer: Listen, nobody talks to *me* like that!

Mechanic: One more time . . . let's go see the manager.

Customer: The only person I'm going to see is my lawyer, and believe me, I'm going to have a *lot* to say to *her*!

Even if CUSTOMER does go to court, does win the lawsuit, does get the car repaired properly at a proper price, this is a confrontation that has been won by MECHANIC. CUSTOMER has done everything wrong, and even if it's true that MECHANIC has tried to charge for unnecessary repairs, it is CUSTOMER who will be without a car while the repairs are going on. It is also CUSTOMER who will have to spend time in court instead of going to work or to school or taking the kids to the beach. The fact that MECHANIC is also being inconvenienced during this is not going to cancel out all that time and money and effort wasted. Only as a last resort is a script like the preceding one justified. (MECHANIC's next line, by the way, would have gone like this: "Suit yourself.")

Mechanic: *Some* skilled mechanics would consider it a real insult if a customer came back and insinuated that work had been done on their car that wasn't really necessary.

Customer: How nice to know that you're not one of those, Mr. Granger.

Mechanic: Oh, I see. You're not going to play that game.

Customer: No. I'm afraid not. Now, let's take a look at that bill again, please.

This is expertly done, and very risky. CUSTOMER should try this only if he or she knows the work of a mechanic upside down and backwards and is prepared to prove it. If you happen to be in that fortunate position, you can afford to try this. Not otherwise. A Leveling challenge with a mechanic, a carpenter, or a skilled craftsman of any kind is appropriate if your skill is at the same level. In that case, by all means go ahead.

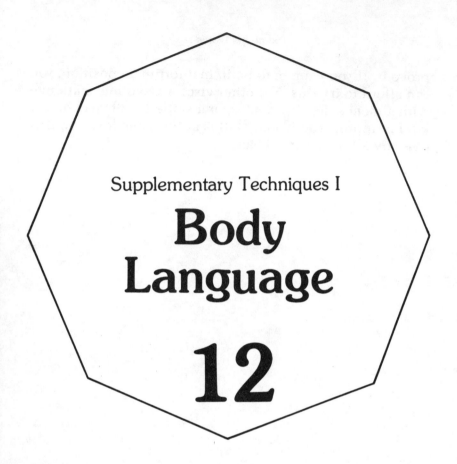

Supplementary Techniques I

Body Language

12

Until now this manual has focused on one specific element of verbal interaction: the sequence of words that is the utterance itself. We've used this artifical separation of words from their contexts for two purposes: (a) to let us look at surface patterns that occur in utterances; and (b) to simplify the process of relating to those surface patterns the unspoken presuppositions that lie behind them.

This has been useful, but it cannot go on forever, since in real life we do not carry on conversations that have no context. For any utterance there will be (a) the verbal channel represented by the words; and (b) at the same time, a *nonverbal* channel that underlies the words and must be considered just as thoroughly in verbal self-defense. (The fact that ideally this underlying nonverbal channel would include the entire real world does not make life—or this book—any simpler.)

Massive amounts of research indicate that when the verbal channel and the nonverbal channel are in conflict and you have no solid information to tell you which one is reliable, the right strategy is to choose the nonverbal. (An example of verbal-nonverbal channel conflict, first pointed out to me by John Grinder and which I have seen many times since then, is the person who says, "I love her so much, there's nothing I wouldn't do for her!" while pounding his fist on the nearest surface and slowly shaking his head from side to side.)

The nonverbal channel is made up of so many different things that its study has spawned a whole set of technical terms in communications fields and in linguistics. You will read of *kinesics, proxemics, pragmatics, paralinguistics,* and so on. None of these terms is exactly right for this chapter; but then, the term I have chosen—*body language*—is not exactly right either. I selected it because it is a familiar term and does cover in a rough way what will be discussed here. However, as used in much recent popular literature, it refers only to gestures, posture, and facial expression; I will be using it more broadly than that. Let us understand it to mean the fullest extension of the phrase "the language of the body," the entire nonverbal channel as it is put to use in verbal interaction. It will then include, for the purposes of this book, not only gestures, posture, and facial expressions but many other things as well. For example, it will include the inflection and quality of the voice, the distance between speaker(s) and listener(s), the messages conveyed by the way a speaker chooses to clothe or decorate the body, the method a speaker uses to decide when it is his or her turn to talk, and so on.

Because doing this topic justice would require a separate book, I am going to concentrate my attention on three specific areas of body language that are both useful in verbal self-defense and suitable for a beginner's manual. (You'll find suggested readings at the end of the chapter to lead you into more advanced material if you want to explore it further.) First, there is the proper use of the voice itself as an *instrument* for producing words, just as you would talk of the proper use of a musical instrument to produce a melody. Then there is the proper arrangement of the parts of the body, including the face, and their best positioning in relation to the physical setting and other person(s) involved in the verbal interaction. Finally, I want to talk about *mannerisms,* nonverbal habits that may either be deliberate or that a speaker may be unaware of. In terms of techniques that can be quickly mastered for maximum positive effect, these three areas are the most promising.

PROPER USE OF THE VOICE

Voice "quality" is a mysterious thing. It involves pitch and nasality and volume and breathiness and harshness and timbre ("timbre" being that even more mysterious quality that lets you know if the instrument you hear being played is a violin or a flute or a piano) and on far into the acoustic night. Experts called phoneticians can tell you more than you'll ever want to know about all of these things, but learning to control each one of them consciously and blend all those separate controls into a natural whole is probably impossible. Fortunately, it needn't be possible. You don't have to know consciously what adjustments to make in muscles and nerves and joints in order to walk. Like the centipede who was doing fine until somebody told her that she had one hundred separate legs to manage, an attempt at such conscious knowledge would only make you fall down. You make all the necessary adjustments without "knowing" what you are doing, and your body has the same skill available for use of the voice as it does for use of the legs and feet.

This is fortunate, because—although it is utterly unjust to do so—people judge other people on the basis of their voice quality, often without taking anything else into account. If your voice is perceived by others as "whiny," perhaps because it is high and nasal and thin, your utterances are going to be perceived that way, too—and your personality. If your voice is perceived as gruff and harsh, you are likely to be considered a bully; if it is breathless and badly controlled, people will assume that you are slightly feather-headed and untrustworthy. The situation *should not be this way;* people should not automatically label others on the basis of voice quality, any more than they should judge them on the basis of such things as haircut or accent or clothing. All these things may have no relationship to the words being said or the kind of person saying them. But as Robert Day said in a brilliant *New Yorker* cartoon in 1970: we are in a real world, in which we cannot change the channel. You, as a student of verbal self-defense, can make a real effort not to do this kind of labeling. You can withhold your judgment of others until you have some better information to base it on than voice quality alone. But you cannot safely assume, ever, that other people will pay you that same courtesy. Therefore, knowing how your voice sounds to others is a crucial part of your self-defense skills, and a pleasant voice quality is as important to your success as the mastery of any technique we have discussed so far. (It would not be an overstatement to say that getting rid of an *unpleasant* voice quality is even more important than any of the other techniques, since it can in fact invalidate all the rest of your skills.)

Begin by listening to a tape recording of your voice in ordinary conversation with a friend. You don't want a distorted or defective tape, of course; however, high fidelity is not important. The inexpensive cassette recorders and tapes you can pick up at the drugstore are more than adequate. Remember that when people listen to you talking they don't get high fidelity either, and what you want to know is how you sound under ordinary conditions, not in a recording studio. Your tape should be at least half an hour long, to give you and your friend a chance to get over feeling self-conscious about the recording process and to start speaking naturally.

My personal experience is that when people hear themselves on a tape, unless they're accustomed to doing so, they immediately declare that that is *not* how they sound. Some of this is an acoustic matter; but for the most part the problem is that the voice they hear does not fit their personal image of the way they sound. Since it is possible that the tape could be defective or the batteries low or something of the kind, if you have this reaction by all means get a second opinion. Ask someone who is used to hearing you talk if the recording sounds like you to them or not. But unless there really is a mechanical problem, 99 out of 100 times what you are hearing is the way you sound to other people—which is what you're trying to find out. Knowing that you sound like Lauren Bacall or Paul Newman to your *self* is a useless piece of information unless other people share that perception, and it is in fact a dangerous illusion that you should get rid of as rapidly as possible. If you are convinced that you sound like Paul Newman, but other people hear you as someone with a high, squeaky voice, one of your major problems in communication has been identified.

What if you find out that the quality of your voice *is* unpleasant? Then what? Rarely, that unpleasantness will be an actual speech disability requiring the attention of a medical expert or a speech therapist. If that's what you're up against, try to get the expert help you need, because it will be worth every penny. People tend to quickly forget minor physical differences from the norm; once they've noticed that you have something they perceive as a "big" nose or a "poor complexion," they get used to it and disregard it. Deciding whether something of that sort requires medical correction is a cosmetic decision, usually. Your voice, however doesn't share that "fading perception" effect. Instead, the more you talk, the more aware people become of whatever it is they find unpleasant, and the greater the handicap it is to your success in communicating with them. This is a serious problem.

Let's assume (as will ordinarily be true) that the problem is not a genuine disability. In that case, I am happy to be able to tell you that there is something you can do about it, that it won't require you to spend huge sums on a voice coach, and that you can begin working on it at once.

First, get it straight in your own mind that your goal is to sound like *your own self*, but with a pleasant voice quality. I warn you about this because the technique I'm about to describe would indeed allow you to train yourself to sound like Lauren Bacall or Paul Newman, and that would be a fatal mistake. It would only make people consider you some kind of nut who thought Lauren Bacall-Paul Newman imitations were appropriate for ordinary conversation.

Second, buy or borrow or rent or check out from a language lab one of those inexpensive cassette recorders I mentioned before, plus about five hours' worth of inexpensive blank tapes. (As of this writing, in 1979, you can buy all of this for about twenty dollars.)

Now, find a friend whose voice quality *you* perceive as pleasant, who is of the same sex and generation as you are, and who is willing to help you out. Have your friend fill all but one of your tapes with ordinary speech—which does not mean reading aloud. Ask for a tape on "The Teacher I Hated Most When I Was a Kid" and one on "Why I Don't/Do Like the President" and "My Most Embarrassing Experience" and so on. Ordinary, talking-to-somebody-else talking. Keep the last of your tapes for your own use, because you will need it for recording your own voice and listening to it to check your progress.

You will work with your tapes in privacy and at your own convenience. How fast you do this is up to you. But *how* you do it is not up to you at all. It must be done *right*, and I'm going to be very autocratic about that, since the chances are that many of the things you have been told about working with such tapes are wrong.

Do *not* listen to a sentence on your friend's tape, stop the tape, repeat the sentence (trying to sound like the one on the tape), and then do that over and over again. The effect of that technique is merely to train you even more thoroughly than you were trained before in your present bad habits. You'll get nowhere that way, because that's not how your brain and your ears and your speech mechanisms work. Instead, pick any sentence (or shorter sequence) on the tape that you want to work with, listen to it several times, and then try to say the sequence ALONG WITH THE TAPE. Do that over and over again, until you can do it easily; then choose a new sequence and go on to work with it. Be sure that you don't write down the sequence and read it back with the tape—reading aloud will never produce natural speech.

Why does this work? Because as you try to speak along with the tape, you will unconsciously hear tiny differences between your own speech and the speech you're using as a model. Differences of volume, pitch, timbre, and so on. You will then try to *reduce* those differences, making use of the constant feedback between the two streams of sound, with your brain going, "Now that's closer on the pitch, but let's turn the volume down a bit . . . yeah, that's better, but now there's too much nasal in there, let's cut that back . . . better, but there's still a difference . . . let me see, how about putting the volume back *up* a tad . . . yeah . . . " and so on. Consciously, you cannot do this; and I am not seriously suggesting that there is any unconscious level at which your "brain" is actually running through that monologue—it's just a way of explaining what is happening without going into a lecture on neurolinguistics, the anatomy of perception and neuroanatomy, and so on. Unconsciously, if you trust yourself and let the mechanisms of your body take over the job, you *can* do this. You will gradually reduce the differences between the tape and your own speech, a little at a time, until they are a good match. (And if you go on fiendishly at this, you can keep it up until they are a *perfect* match. At which point you have trained yourself to sound like an imitation of your friend. Remember, this is not your goal.)

Once a week do another tape of yourself talking for twenty minutes or so, and listen to it. When your voice quality begins to sound pleasant, STOP. You have gone far enough. If you're not sure you can trust your judgment and think you may just have become so accustomed to the way you sound on tape that you imagine all is well, get a second opinion again. Chances are that you have indeed fixed your problem. Thereafter you need only check once in a while to be sure you haven't gone back to your old bad habits—once a month for six months, and maybe once more six months later. This should be sufficient.

Before we leave proper use of the voice, I want to take up briefly the topic of stress. This has been mentioned before—for instance, when I have pointed out that the difference between a verbal attack and the neutral utterance of a Leveler is often the presence or absence of stress on a word such as "really." But stress is so very important, since it actually changes the meaning of the words you use, that I think it requires further explanation. The classic example type from linguistics, used by everyone but first pointed out by Edward Klima, goes like this:

1. "What are we having for dinner, Daddy?"
2. "What are we having for dinner—*Daddy?*"

(There's a pause in the second example, but it is the stress that really matters.) Sentence 1 asks Daddy what the dinner menu will be, and sentence 2 asks somebody else whether Daddy is going to be the main course. That's a big difference in meaning to be riding on stress alone, but English works that way. In fact, one of the quickest ways a native speaker of another language can spot native English speakers is by their habit of using English stress in every language they learn, whether the other language has that characteristic or not. French, for example, does *not* have emphatic stress, but Americans rarely let that stand in their way when they speak French.

Stress is heard as either higher pitch or greater volume or both. It must be handled with great care, since in English its function is to call attention to some part of an utterance, and since it *always* brings with it presuppositions that may or may not be reflected on the surface. Look at the following set of sentences, with their meanings spelled out beneath them in a very exaggerated way for clarity:

3. a. "John is the only man in the room." (Neutral statement of fact, meaning "This room contains only one male human being, and that male human being is the individual referred to by the name John.")
b. "*John* is the only man in the room." ("John—not the other person or persons I just heard you mention—is the only male human being in the room, in my opinion.")

c. "John *is* the only man in the room." ("John—despite the statement made by another person or persons to the contrary—is the only male human being in the room, in my opinion.")
d. "John is *the* only man in the room." (Mystery utterance. The only likely context is a teacher correcting a pupil who has read the sentence aloud as "John is that only man in the room," or something similar.)
e. "John is the *only* man in the room." ("This room contains only one male human being, in my opinion, and that male human being is the individual named John; and I want to be sure that you realize that there is no other male human being present in the room. This *remains* my opinion, even if there are other human beings in the room who, as a neutral statement of fact, might be referred to by others as 'men.'")
f. "John is the only *man* in the room." ("This room contains only one male human being, whose name is John, and that is my opinion regardless of whether there is anyone or anything else whatsoever in the room; John, and uniquely John, meets my personal specifications for a male human being.")
g. "John is the only man *in* the room." ("There may be male human beings who are outside the room, or near it in some other way, but the only one actually located inside the room itself, in my opinion, is John.")
h. "John is the only man in *the* room." (See example (d)—it's one of those.)
i. "John is the only man in the *room*." ("There may be male human beings in the car or in the basement or somewhere else, but in my opinion the only male human being actually in the room itself is John, and I want you to be aware that it is my opinion, because I consider it important.")

That constitutes a linguistic demonstration of the power, and the danger, of English stress. If it doesn't convince you, you probably cannot be convinced. You are like the karate student who has been shown the technique for breaking a brick with the side of the hand but believes it is a trick, and you are likely to be vulnerable to people who know better.

Whenever you hear emphatic stress in an utterance, take the time to listen *hard.* And then expand that utterance into everything you can tell it means, as I have done beneath the examples in sentence 3. If you don't have time to do this in conversations, try to jot down the sentence to analyze later when you are not pressed. With practice you will learn to do this as rapidly as any other kind of verbal processing, and with the same lack of conscious attention. And learn to give the same careful attention to your own use of stress. It matters.

PROPER PLACEMENT OF THE BODY

One of the biggest dangers for the novice in verbal self-defense lies in the oversimplification of the subject that has found its way into many recent books and magazines. This is an unavoidable problem; I myself have had to oversimplify time and time again in the present book, and experts will be criticizing me for that. But a book that can be understood only if you already have an advanced degree in the subject is of no use to the beginner, and refusing to try to make things clear because of what is called "stooping to popularization" is a position that tends to make ignorance a permanent condition. I don't approve of it. (And notice, please, that I said "ignorance," not "stupidity." There is a great difference.) Someone with a Ph.D. in biology may be totally ignorant about anthropology, as well as about car mechanics, cooking, the geography of Sri Lanka, and many other things outside his or her professional specialty. It takes enormous amounts of time to keep up with the one field that is your career or avocation, and for you to be ignorant of most other fields is not only not a disgrace, it is inevitable.

All that I can do here is caution you not to take for granted everything you read about body language. The idea that a particular set of gestures, a particular way of crossing the feet or legs, a particular way of wrinkling the forehead, can be relied upon to have the same meaning all the time in every person you encounter is a myth. People who write books on the subject rarely mean to give that impression and can usually be counted on to tell you that they are talking about most of the people in a specific cultural or ethnic group, most of the time. But magazine articles, quick spots on television talk shows or news programs, newspaper stories and reviews with quotes taken out of context, as well as speeches by "instant experts," all tend to overlook these warnings. You get the idea that you can memorize a list of gestures, expressions, and postures along with a list of their "meanings" and then rely on that universally. This is totally false. You cannot even rely on such a list for *one* person in a single culture all of the time. The gesture that means "peace" or "victory" to Anglo Americans, depending on their age, means a number of radically different things to other ethnic groups, and using it indiscriminately is an excellent way to make a bad impression. *Never* use a nonverbal item cross-culturally without checking it out first, to the extent that such things are under your control.

One of the primary reasons why Computer Mode is the safest possible stance for the beginner is that it is the mode with the fewest gestures, the least change in facial expression, and so on. That doesn't mean it has no dangers at all on the nonverbal channel, but it is the least dangerous of the Satir Modes you could choose while you are learning.

Be sensitive to distance—the size of the personal space that other people want to have around them. It varies from one group to another. Some studies have reported that people who are violent in their behavior require a larger personal space than the one that is typical even for their own group; if research proves that to be true, it will be important knowledge, and it is worth taking seriously even at this stage. Much research shows that Latinos need a smaller personal space than do Anglos, which leads to many incidents in which the Latino keeps trying to move closer as the Anglo keeps trying to move away, and the end result is an Anglo with back to the wall because he or she cannot back up any farther.

Since you cannot possibly know what the favored personal space of every individual you talk to will be, you need a general technique to help you in every situation to some degree—a rough rule of thumb. It goes like this: If the person you're talking to keeps moving closer to you, making you feel a little crowded, assume that that person needs a smaller personal space than you do for conversation, and *hold still.* If he or she then stops moving in on you, you've made the right decision, and things will go better, provided that you can master your own feeling of being hemmed in. Conversely, if the person you're talking to keeps backing up, assume that he or she needs a bigger personal space than you require, and stop trying to get closer. If you're right, again things will improve. Notice that in both cases the remedy is to hold still and let the other person set the limits of the space for your conversation. Remember what you did, remember how it worked (or didn't work), and add it to your records. Don't make the mistake of assuming that it will always work for another person of that particular ethnic group, age group, sex, or other identifying characteristic; but make a note that will help you spot rough general patterns for later use.

Finally, be aware that the way you deck out your body

and where you put it (and the way anybody does those things) is a very large chunk of the meaning in any verbal interaction. You have every right to go to a job interview for a junior executive position with the IBM Corporation wearing your hair loose to your waist (whatever your sex), a full beard or no bra (whichever fits your situation), and no shoes. That is your moral right, and nobody is entitled to take it away from you. Similarly, you have the right to sit slouched in your chair through that interview, staring at the ceiling, if you want to. But it is stupid (and notice, this time I said *stupid,* not ignorant) to be unaware that by making the decision to do this you are delivering a lengthy message. It runs something like this, on the nonverbal channel:

> "Okay, here I am. I know what an IBM junior executive is supposed to look like, but I don't happen to give a damn. This is how I look, this is the way I prefer to look, and whether you like the way I look is of no interest to me. If you want to hire me, you hire me like this, because this is how I am, and you might just as well know it right from the start."

You may be so good that that message will get you hired. The personnel person may be overwhelmed by your rugged individualism, your honesty, your courage, your outstanding record, or some combination of these. But be aware that you are saying all of that, even if every overt word you say is in a nice polite "Yes, sir/No, sir" style, and that the full message will be heard.

If you don't care to deliver that message, there is another rule of thumb you should observe. Do a little research before you go into a verbal interaction. Find out what your audience usually looks like by looking at some other people who are part of it and observing what they ordinarily wear and how they ordinarily take up a position in conversation. Let that be your guide, to whatever limit you are willing to make such adjustments. In an advanced book on verbal self-defense, I would go into methods for breaking the rules and getting away with it, because that is possible. But we don't have room for that here.

MANNERISMS

A mannerism, in the context of this book, is a verbal habit. A striking and obvious example of a mannerism is the use of multiple emphatic stresses in a single utterance, like this:

> "If you *really* mean what you *say* about student *rights,* then you won't *make* us write term papers if we don't *want* to."

For someone to use stress in this fashion is as irritating as if he or she continually hummed under his breath or cracked his knuckles. It is typical only of small children and of adults who do not mind being considered childish, and it is maddening. Stress is intended, you will recall, to focus attention on a particular part of an utterance. When attention is focused in half a dozen different places, it becomes impossible to make sense of the utterance or to know what matters to the speaker, and this provokes either anger or indifference. Two uses of stress within one utterance of ordinary length is about the upper limit; and if every sentence used has some stressed element, the eventual effect is about the same as multiple stress in one sentence. Stress must be used sparingly and only when it is truly necessary.

Another example is the gesture so many teachers have, at all levels—that of shaking their index finger at someone while the rest of the hand makes a fist. Teachers may start out doing this deliberately, but by the time they have taught for ten years, it has frequently become a habit of which they are no longer aware. It is a threatening gesture and is only appropriate when a threat is needed. A standard progression is for a new teacher to use the gesture in a kindergarten to convince a child that he or she is NOT going to be allowed to hit other students with the building blocks—that is appropriate. Ten years later that same teacher, talking to a close friend at lunch about almost any subject, is shaking that finger nonstop—that is not appropriate. In teachers of retirement age it tends to become something they do even when they are talking to themselves or talking on the telephone, which is hilarious. I tell the teachers I am training that this particular mannerism is so dangerous, and so sneaky, that you must simply decide at the beginning that you will never use it, and stick to that. Even if it means that at first you have to clasp your hands behind your back to keep from using it (which may be necessary if you've already acquired it as a habit or if you "don't know what to do with your hands"). Of the two mannerisms, the one with hands behind the back is by far the lesser of two evils, and with any luck you'll be able to abandon that as well.

To break yourself of *any* mannerism, by the way, this is the rule of thumb: Choose some neutral Computer Mode position that won't allow you to do whatever the mannerism requires and use that to break yourself of the bad habit. Try not to acquire the Computer Mode position as a new mannerism; this is an obvious danger. Nevertheless, I will defend to the last fall the proposition that if you must have bad nonverbal habits, those in Computer Mode are the best bad ones to have.

As was true for judging personal space on the spot and without any extra information, you handle this by paying very careful attention; by writing down and analyzing what you observe, in order to record general patterns; and by letting the other person determine the limits so far as is possible. If the other person is shaking his or her finger at you constantly in that Teacher Gesture, assume that it is a mannerism and *cancel* your automatic "Hey, I'm being threatened!" response. Don't retaliate with threatening stuff of your own. If *you* are doing the finger shaking and the other person is becoming annoyed, have sense and skill enough to realize what is happening and stop. If you don't know what it is about your nonverbal behavior that is causing the trouble but you notice that the atmosphere is heating up, try assuming full Computer Mode as a safe beginning stance and maintain that until you have more information available. (A word of warning: you will find books and articles that tell you to work with this problem, and other problems of body language, by matching your own body language to that of the person you're dealing with. This is an extremely powerful technique, and it can be taught. But it is for experts, not beginners. If you fumble it—for example, if you cause the other person to think that you are mocking him or her—you'll be in trouble. *Not* recommended.)

The major characteristics of the Computer Mode nonverbal channel, for most Americans, will be the following:

1. very few gestures, or none at all
2. very little facial expression—the absolute minimum that can be used without giving the impression that you aren't listening at all
3. very little change in body language; that is, whatever position and expression the Computer starts out with is maintained almost without alteration throughout the conversation
4. never any sudden movement or change of expression or posture—everything is done calmly, slowly, and without surface evidence of emotion
5. never any body language that is typical of the other Satir Modes; that is, no Blamer body language, such as pounding

fists or shaking fingers, no Placater body language, such as whining or crying or wringing the hands, and no Distracter body language, such as wiggling or constantly fooling with your hair or your glasses or your clothes. (Leveler body language cannot be predicted, by the way.)

Watch out for mannerisms that represent an "in" joke, if you can. For example, the gesture that marks you as an amateur in a personnel interview for a junior executive position—thus costing you points—is the one where you reach up with one hand, taking off your glasses by the earpiece, hold the glasses in the area around your chin, and stare intently into the interviewer's eyes as you say something. The more you do this, the funnier it will become to the personnel manager, who will suspect (probably accurately) that you read about that somewhere or saw it on a talk show and that you don't know what you're doing.

These come and go, unfortunately, and what is effective in April may be funny in May and effective again in June. *Watch* the person you're talking with. If he or she reacts to some mannerism by what looks like a struggle not to laugh, it's a good idea to give it up at once. (A really skilled interviewer won't be this transparent, but you can try.)

Avoid interpreting another person's mannerisms categorically, in terms of an unquestioned Popular Wisdom. For instance, most Anglos have been brought up to believe something roughly like this: "All people who cannot look you in the eye are dishonest." If, from the perspective of your own cultural group, there is a violent clash here—say, "All people who insist on looking you right in the eye are rude"—trouble is clearly possible. You'll avoid direct eye contact because you don't want to be thought rude, and the other person will assume that you're unable to look him or her in the eye because you're not honest. What makes this dangerous rather than trivial is that usually neither one of you is aware of what's happening. The other person turns you down or doesn't hire you on "an intuitive feeling that you just aren't the right person" for whatever you were there for. You decide that this happened because the other person is prejudiced against your particular race, sex, age, life-style, or whatever is *your* most common "intuitive feeling" about these things. You're both wrong, the verbal transaction was a flop, and the whole process has just been reinforced in both of you in such a way that it will go on happening.

Whichever side of the confrontation you are on, use as a rule of thumb the same one I've been giving throughout this chapter: PAY ATTENTION AND DON'T LEAP TO CONCLUSIONS. Give the other person the benefit of the doubt until you have information to work with.

This chapter is already a long and heavy one, and it's time to wind it up. I want to tackle the problem of the idea that all these things are somehow a massive compromise of your principles. In my workshops and seminars people say that they would be "prostituting themselves," that they refuse to "suck up" to other people (or "talk down" to other people, depending on their status) in these ways. This is a gross misunderstanding of what you are doing and needs to be straightened out.

In verbal self-defense, the ideal—the undoubtedly unattainable ideal—is never to have to use what you know because all confrontations are headed off before they start and only Leveling takes place. Not because you are a gutless wonder, but because you know what you are doing. A major factor in working toward that goal is the ability to *reduce tension* in any kind of verbal interaction. All of the techniques I've been discussing in this chapter are for that purpose—lowering the level of tension and emotion in verbal encounters so that a move up to Leveling can become a possibility. They are not techniques for verbal self-prostitution; they are defusing techniques. They require great skill and carry with them great honor.

REFERENCES AND SUGGESTED READINGS

Books:

BIRDWHISTELL, RAY L. *Kinesics and Context*. Philadelphia: University of Pennsylvania Press, 1970. (This is a scholarly book but is not overly technical; it is perhaps the major work in this field.)

FAST, JULIUS. *Body Language*. Philadelphia: M. Evans & Company, Inc., 1970. (A popular treatment of the subject.)

HENLEY, NANCY. *Body Politics: Power, Sex, and Nonverbal Communication*. Englewood Cliffs, NJ.: Prentice-Hall, Inc., 1977.

NIERENBERG, GERARD I., and HENRY H. CALERO. *How to Read a Person Like a Book*. New York: Pocket Books, 1971. (Another popular treatment.)

Articles:

FISHER, SEYMOUR. "Experiencing Your Body: You Are What You Feel." *Saturday Review of Science*, July 8, 1972, pp. 27–32. (This article deals in detail with male and female perceptions of body image. Highly recommended.)

LONGFELLOW, L. "Body Talk: The Game of Feeling and Expression." *Psychology Today*, October 1970, pp. 45–55.

STEIN, HARRY. "How to Tell a Joke If You're Not Alan King." *Esquire*, November 7, 1973, pp. 86–87. (In the same issue and by the same author, "How to Imitate Bogart If You're Not Rich Little.")

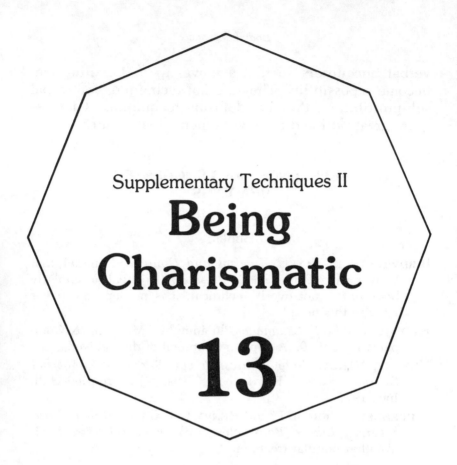

Supplementary Techniques II

Being Charismatic

13

"Charisma"—one of the mystery words. People are said to "have" charisma in the same way that they "have" black eyes. Charisma is viewed as something with which you are born, a gift from the Fates, and something as inseparably a part of you as your eyes and heart. Definitions of charisma are not very illuminating; a fair summary would be something like this: Charisma is a mysterious, irresistible, almost magical ability to make others believe you and want to do anything you ask of them.

If you are believed because of the logic of what you say, that is not charisma. Furthermore, there is a libraryful of research to indicate that logic is almost useless as a way of convincing people of anything. (You might consider the "logic" of convincing women to buy a cosmetic because it is so natural looking that when you wear it nobody can tell that you are doing so; that's an interesting example of the principle.)

If people do what you ask them to do simply because you have the power to force them to—with a gun or a whip or a spanking or a failing grade or a three-week assignment to latrine duty—that's not charisma. The crucial difference between coercion and charisma is that you *want* to believe the charismatic individual and you want to do anything he or she asks of you, and you don't care at all about other factors. It's said that Adlai Stevenson, when complimented on a speech, once pointed out that people often said what nice speeches he made, but that after John F. Kennedy's speeches they said, "Let's march!" *That* is charisma.

Charisma is a matter of perception. In the discussion of English stress in Chapter Twelve, I told you that it is heard as higher pitch and louder volume; experts in acoustics and phonetics would tell you that that's a mighty inadequate description of what stress actually is. For the purpose of verbal self-defense, however, it is that perception that is crucial, and that triggers the responses in the hearer that make stress so tricky a matter. Charisma, too, whatever its scientific explanation might be, is *perceived*—seen and heard and felt—as the ability to convince and compel without force. And it is that perception that concerns us here. The interesting question is: Can you be taught to bring about that perception in people listening to you? I am prepared to claim that you can be.

Nobody has ever developed a test to measure someone's Charisma Quotient, to my knowledge. But if we had one, every technique you have learned from this book so far is guaranteed to raise your CQ a little bit, and every technique yet to come will continue that process. Just how high you can go on the charisma scale will depend on many things, some of which are indeed a matter of the Fates. No question about it, it helps a lot to have been born physically attractive, in glorious health, and wealthy. The one thing that genuinely matters, however, is how hard you are willing to work at it.

A warning—don't confuse charisma with Leveling. The two may overlap. The person trapped in an elevator, thinking he's scared, looking like he's scared, and saying he's scared, is Leveling; whether he's also charismatic is something you cannot know unless you are there to judge. Similarly, the saleswoman who knows that the car she's selling you is a bad buy, but who uses both her verbal and her nonverbal channels to convince you that the opportunity to buy it is something you should be grateful for, is clearly charismatic, but she is not Leveling. In the chapter on emergency techniques we'll take on the problem of how to spot and deal with that most dangerous of communicating humans, the phony Leveler. In this chapter we are going to look at several techniques for being charismatic that can be learned at the beginner's level and that will give you a good return on your investment of effort.

PREFERRED SENSORY MODES

Over the years many researchers have noted that people seem to have individual preferences for the use of one kind of sensory information over another. This research has concentrated most heavily on vision and hearing, although recently more attention has been paid to touch, taste, and smell. To my knowledge, John Grinder and Richard Bandler were the first to publish work on the way in which people demonstrate these preferences in their language patterns, and their initial research has been developed extensively by their associates. Here I will touch on only one very limited aspect of this subject, one that can be an extremely useful addition to your verbal self-defense techniques.

If we assume that it is usual for people to prefer one sensory mode to another and agree that they will often make their preference clear in their language, we can set up a list of examples such as the following:

- *Sight:* "I see what you mean. I see your point."
  "That's very clear."
  "That looks good to me."
- *Hearing:* "I hear what you're trying to say."
  "What you're saying is just a lot of noise to me."
  "That sounds fine to me."
- *Touch:* "Somehow this situation just doesn't feel right."
  "I can't put my finger on the problem."
  "It feels okay to me."
- *Smell:* "This is a very fishy situation, if you ask me."
  "The whole thing smells rotten to me."
  "I'll sniff around and find out what's going on."
- *Taste:* "The whole thing leaves a bad taste in my mouth."
  "I can almost taste what's wrong here, but I don't know how to explain it."
  "This really sickens me."

The last two sensory modes, smell and taste, seem to be more rare as preferred modes than the first three. (And they are often treated as a single mode, because physiologically they are closely connected.) This may be because so few people develop these senses to any extent—exceptions would be perfume specialists and wine tasters—or it may be due to a lack of English vocabulary items for expressing them, or both. Or there may be a quite different explanation. Much more research will have to be done in order to settle this question.

For our purposes what is important is the technique of matching the sensory mode being used by the person you are talking with. Look at these two brief exchanges:

X: That's my proposal. Now I'd like to know if it's clear, and if you see any problems.

Y: No, it really looks good to me.
(Sensory modes match.)

X: That's my proposal. Now I'd like to know if it's clear, and if you see any problems.

Y: No, it really sounds fine to me.
(Sensory modes clash.)

Although both of *Y's* responses "mean" the same thing—both express approval—they differ in that one uses sensory mode matching, and the other does not. This is not trivial, particularly in a verbal situation for which a confrontation atmosphere can be predicted in advance. (For example, a meeting between management and labor or a court trial.) Often you can use this technique unobtrusively as a way of keeping the level of tension in a discussion lower than it might otherwise be, and the minimal effort involved is well worth the result. Look at the following example:

CONFRONTATION TWENTY-FOUR

Teacher: Look, Bill, your problem in school is no mystery. It's obvious—anybody can see that you just don't try.

Bill: I do too try! I work on it all the time. I just don't *get* it, that's all!

Teacher: Bill . . . come on, now! Your spelling, for instance. Do you really expect me to believe that you study those words the way you're supposed to—*really* study them—and still miss almost every one on your tests? I'm not blind, you know, *or* stupid.

Bill: And I suppose I'm both. And a liar, too.

Teacher: I didn't say that.

Bill: Well, that's how what you're saying makes me feel.

Teacher: Bill, you have got to try not to see everything I do to help you as a personal attack. That's a very warped way of looking at things.

Bill: Now I'm crazy, too—thanks a lot.

Teacher: You see? With that attitude, there is no way anybody can help you!

Bill: Okay, okay! I give up!

Teacher: Like I said—and now you've agreed with me—it's not that you can't do the work, it's that you *won't*. I hope you see the difference.

This teacher, who has used visual sensory words exclusively while the student has used only words of touch, now has a totally hostile and alienated young man to deal with. BILL is of course convinced that TEACHER has no respect for him at all—which may or may not be true.

We would be far beyond oversimplification and into the land of fairy tales if I gave you the impression that I thought sensory mode matching was a cure for every problem. Or that it would have automatically eliminated the difficulties between BILL and TEACHER. Not only is that not guaranteed, but the technique must be used with discretion; if you overdo it, you risk making your listener feel that you are somehow mimicking him or her. Done properly, however, sensory mode matching is a powerful way to reduce potential conflict. It makes your listener feel that the two of you are "on the same wavelength" or "share the same perceptions," that you are an unusually understanding and empathic person, and that you are a pleasure to talk to. (In short, it makes you more charismatic.)

Learning to do this quickly and naturally requires practice. You should plan to add it to your Journal work, because you will need to do some advance practice before you try it in real-life situations. First, find out what your own preferred sensory mode is by paying attention to the language you yourself use. Then practice identifying the preferred sensory modes of other people by paying close attention to their language patterns. Finally, practice translating utterances from one sensory mode to another.

To do this, you will need to be aware of predicates; for the most part, that is where you will find your clues. English has four kinds of predicates, as in the example sentences that follow, where the predicate is everything to the right of the dot in the sentence.

ENGLISH PREDICATES:

- True verbs: "Tracy • worked, left, sang." (A true verb can always have "-ing" added to it.)
- Adjectives: "Tracy • is tall, short, tired."
- Identifiers: "Tracy • is a teacher, doctor, friend."
- [Locations in space: "Tracy • is in the kitchen, in Paris."
- Locations in time: "The party • is at six, is on Tuesday."]

Any predicate that fits into a particular sensory mode is a clue to the preferences of the speaker; the more frequently you hear him or her use predicates from that sensory mode, the more you can be sure that it is the preferred one.

The list that follows will give you a few examples of predicates from each sensory mode. Be prepared for a shortage of vocabulary in the Smell and Taste sets, as well as frequent overlaps. (This mirrors the situation in your body when your food tastes odd to you if you have a stuffy nose from a cold or hay fever.)

- *Sight:* see, look, glance, observe, notice, watch, appear, seem, resemble, be clear, be transparent, be invisible, be obvious, be lucid, be foggy, be muggy, see right through (X), have not even a shadow of a problem with (X), clear everything up, have an eagle eye
- *Hearing:* hear, listen, pay attention to what (X) says, be repetitious, be garbled, be full of static, be just a lot of noise, sound fine, sound stupid, be unable to make out what (X) is saying, sound like (X), talk (X) to death, be a gossip
- *Touch:* feel, touch, get, make, grasp, dig, handle, put your finger on (X), get hold of (X), be smooth as silk, be too hot to handle, be slippery, be easy to deal with, be right where you can get down to business, be tickled, be a sneak, be a feeling person, be always pushing people around
- *Smell:* smell, sniff, sniff around, stink, be rotten, be nosy, be a stinking person, smell like (X), be where nothing smells right
- *Taste:* taste, gobble, be nasty, be sweet, be right on the tip of your tongue, make you nauseated, make you sick, be sour, be enough to gag a maggot, be in a sickening place

Now for the "translation" exercise. You don't have to be a fanatic about this. Perfect matches like the following set are rare:

That looks good to me.
    sounds great
    feels fine
    smells right

Notice that even for an obvious set like this one, we would have to play around with the example to find a rough equivalent for the sensory mode of taste. We could say, "That leaves a good taste in my mouth," but "That tastes right to me" is not a likely sentence except with reference to something you eat or drink.

I'm going to give you ten sentences for practice that are hard enough to constitute a reasonable workout. By the time you finish them, you will have a good grasp of the technique. Here is one more example set to get you started:

- *Sight:* "I don't think you should buy that car. I don't like the looks of the deal, and I don't like the looks of that salesman, either."
- *Hearing:* "I don't think you should buy that car. I don't like the sound of the deal, and I don't like the way that salesman talks, either."
- *Touch:* "I don't think you should buy that car. I have a funny feeling about the whole deal, including that salesman. He really gets to me."
- *Smell:* "I don't think you should buy that car. I think the whole deal smells fishy, and that salesman is a real stinker."
- *Taste:* "I don't think you should buy that car. The whole deal leaves a bad taste in my mouth, and that salesman makes me sick at my stomach."

PRACTICE SENTENCES FOR YOU TO WORK ON:

1. "Maria has a good grasp of the problems involved in starting her own business."
2. "When everything looks rosy, that's the time to be careful."
3. "The mechanic said he wasn't sure he could do much about the transmission, but he'd give it a try."

4. "All the team members understood what the coach was getting at, but following through wouldn't be easy."
5. "The president said we would all have to pull together if we wanted to get anywhere."
6. "I can't see things your way, but I don't think it's because you're not being clear—I think I just don't agree with your ideas."
7. "Ellen said the trip sounded foolish and expensive to her, but if the whole family wanted to be deaf, she didn't intend to try to make them understand."
8. "If you don't get hold of yourself, there's no telling what will happen to you next."
9. "The weather was rotten, the people were rotten, and I could smell the lies ten feet away."
10. "Every time he says that word, it's like I just ate a tuna fish pizza cake."

You may find some predicates impossible to identify, or they may seem to be combinations. (For instance, is "I just can't swallow that" a touch or a taste predicate?) What you are watching for is clear-cut patterns that seem to show a systematic preference, not subtle nuances. You won't find anybody under normal circumstances whose predicates are confined *exclusively* to one sensory mode.

SYSTEMATIC ORGANIZATION OF UTTERANCES

There was a time, and not so very long ago, when what I am about to describe to you next was a part of the education of anyone who went as far as the eighth grade. Nothing I am about to say is new; it is the material of the ancient rhetoric class and was ancient even when Plato was talking about it. Today, however, unless you enroll in a course in making speeches or sermons, you are unlikely to learn even the simplest facts about the rhetoric of oral language. The rhetoric class today is devoted to teaching you how to use written language. This is a serious problem in education at a time when the telephone call has almost eliminated the personal letter, when many people spend their entire working lives without ever needing to write anything that involves more than filling out forms, and when the all-pervasive influence of television has the lion's share of the public's attention.

This book doesn't have space for an entire course in old-fashioned rhetoric. But we can take up three techniques that are easily mastered and that have a high charisma-boosting potential. To begin with, they make you sound as if you know what you are talking about. They give your speech a soothing rhythm that is appealing to the ear, even if you aren't really being listened to (and even if you aren't really saying anything).

I once sat through a forty-minute talk by one of the most charismatic men I know, and I am here to assure you that it had no semantic content whatsoever—it meant nothing at all. He had been scheduled to talk but hadn't bothered to prepare anything and was winging it all the way. When he finished, I expected some expression of outrage from the audience—after all, they had paid to hear him. It didn't happen. Everybody clapped, everybody smiled, and a woman sitting in front of me turned around and said, "I didn't understand a single word he said, but I just *know* it had to be important!" Amazing. That is what happens when people are not taught anything about verbal self-defense.

We're going to take a look at three mechanisms:

parallelism, the unifying metaphor, and culturally loaded vocabulary.

Parallelism

Charismatic speech is always balanced speech. That balance makes it easy to listen to and easy to remember. It makes following the speaker something you can do without effort, because you so quickly catch on to the pattern and know what to expect. The balance also creates that comforting (or stirring) rhythm I mentioned before, to which human beings can be counted on to respond.

One of the easiest ways to work toward this balance is to be certain that whenever you speak of more than one of anything—and especially if you speak of more than two—you use the same language form for each item in the series. For example:

> "I have a goal that will not be ignored. I have a plan that must not be forgotten. I have a vision that cannot be denied."

Now compare this with

> "I have a goal that will not be ignored. The plan that I've worked out is one that everybody must remember. And my vision, now—let them try to deny me *that!*"

Which is more effective, the first or the second version? You may have the feeling that the first version sounds pompous (it does), that it is repetitious (it is), and that the second version is clear and forceful and will make the speaker sound like somebody whose head is on straight. And you may be right. The one that is charismatic, however, the one that would provoke the "Let's march!" rather than "What a nice speech!" reaction, is the first of the two. Notice how carefully it is structured: "I have a . . . [one-syllable noun] . . . that . . . [modal auxiliary] . . . not be . . . [two-or-three syllable verb]."

Using *one* three-syllable verb ("forgotten") between the two two-syllable ones ("ignored" and "denied") is the master touch of slight variety that does not distract from the basic pattern but keeps it from being perceived as overdone. By the time the second sentence has gone by, the listener is relaxed, knows what to expect, and need not pay attention anymore. So long as the pattern is maintained, the perception of the speaker as charismatic will be maintained also—and content has little to do with it. Politicians and expert trial lawyers know this very well, as do people who run encounter groups, and they capitalize on it to the fullest extent. It takes most of the labor out of speech preparation.

Perhaps the most striking proof of this is the recent work of Donald Shields and John Cragan, two social scientists who have programmed an IBM 370 computer to produce a nine-minute political speech that could be used anywhere under any circumstances. The computer's output has resulted in standing ovations, time and time again (which, I hope, should go far to dispel the idea that charisma is an inborn quality granted one by Providence.)

You may never have to make a speech, in the formal sense of the word, although the ability to do so is well worth acquiring. It's very handy to have someone around who can always be counted on to explain to the PTA or the board of directors or the secretarial pool, or any other group, the content of some message that needs to be passed along. If you can also count on that person to carry out this task without fuss and to handle the audience in such a way that it will always be in a pleasant frame of mind afterward, even if the message itself was not pleasant, you are likely to consider that person extremely valuable. It starts with "Miss Kuljak, would you mind going down to Payroll and explaining to them that memo I dictated to you yesterday morning? The supervisor tells me they're upset about it, which means they didn't understand it." And it ends with Miss Kuljak being sent to major conferences in luxurious hotels, at her employer's expense, to represent the firm on the speaker's platform. That's worth remembering.

But even if you have no interest in formal speechmaking, the principle is the same in ordinary daily conversation. All of the following examples are just plain talk, but all use parallelism:

1. "I'm upset, I'm angry, and I'm annoyed." (NOT "I'm upset, and you've made me mad, and I am annoyed, too.")
2. "Pick up your shoes, put away your socks, and turn off that television set." (NOT "Please pick your shoes up. And your socks don't belong there, they belong in the drawer. And *why* do you have the TV on?")
3. "To go to the lake would be fun, and to go to the fair might be interesting—but to go see your mother would be appropriate." (NOT "It would be fun to go to the lake, and going to the fair might be interesting, but I think that for you to go see your mother is the appropriate thing to do.")
4. "If you're worried, say so. If you're scared, tell me about it. And if you're confused, try to explain why." (NOT "If you're worried, say so. Tell me whether you're scared or not. And if I don't know whether you're confused, or why, because you haven't even tried to explain to me, how can I help?")
5. "You can have steak for dinner—and no dessert. You can have salad for dinner—and pie for dessert. Or you can have half a steak for dinner—and melon for dessert. You decide." (NOT "Look, you have to decide. Do you want steak for

dinner? Fine, but then you can't have any dessert. You can only have pie for dessert if you eat *just* salad for your dinner. Or I guess you could have part of a steak, and then have some melon for dessert if you want to.")

There is affirmative parallelism, as in "I will stay, and I will work," and there is negative parallelism, as in "I will neither stay nor work." And if your head is beginning to have echoes in it, along the lines of "If nominated I will not run; if elected I will not serve," fine. That means both that I am accomplishing what I set out to accomplish and that it is time to stop.

The best exercise I can give you for learning about parallelism is to tell you to turn to John F. Kennedy's inaugural address and take it apart, one sentence at a time, noting every parallel structure it contains. (Your public library will have it.) When you get through doing that, you'll know a great deal about parallelism.

The Unifying Metaphor

For a plan of any complexity at all to have a chance of success, particularly if there is opposition to it, one of two things is required: (a) superior force—the machine gun, the raise, the promotion, the scholarship; or (b) a unifying metaphor to be used as a peg to hang the plan on. Advertising agencies, public relations firms, and image makers of all kinds rely on the second alternative. It's less expensive, less complicated, and people don't hate you for it afterward; furthermore, it tends to be self-perpetuating. The unifying metaphor is essential to charismatic speech.

If we had to choose a single most popular Great American Unifying Metaphor, it would unquestionably be the Western Frontier. That one can be used over and over and over again; it never fails. The Marlboro man is its personification. Almost every American (even the American Indian, which is both ironic and mystifying) grows up today watching Westerns on television and in the movies; and the whole elaborate system—a kind of *consensus perception* of reality—is something you can expect to find in almost everyone's memory. Whether any of it is true or logical or any of those good things is irrelevant. (It was in the Western Frontier that guns never ran out of bullets no matter how often you fired them, all Indians spoke the same language and lived in wigwams, and hired killers preferred horses to women. None of that has any logic behind it, but it does not interfere with our consensus perception of the West as having been that way.) That metaphor of the Old West is a perceptual peg, and from it hang a whole lot of things that you don't ever have to mention because they are presupposed by the metaphor. For example:

1. All cowboys were gallant and chaste and would have died rather than betray another cowboy.
2. Daniel Boone.
3. John Wayne.
4. All women who ran saloons were really Earth Mother types, and if you had any problems, you could turn to them.
5. There was always more of everything; you just moved on.
6. Anybody in a black hat was a bad guy.
7. Doctors would ride thirty miles through a blizzard in the middle of the night to take a bullet out of your shoulder, and if you never paid them, that was all right. And the cross way they talked was just to cover up how tender and compassionate they really were.
8. Brave men never cried.
9. Women never smelled bad.
10. No American ever cheated anybody or lied to anybody or stole anything from anybody except (a) those who were

hung for it, and good riddance to them; and (b) those who spent the rest of their lives making it up to those they'd wronged, and God bless *them*.

11. Real men didn't talk much, but they had deep thoughts.
12. The bad guys always lost.
(and so on . . .)

A construct like this is very, very useful. It saves enormous amounts of time, effort, and money. If you can find a unifying metaphor to use as a peg for your proposal, whatever it may be, you can rely on all the presupposed semantic chunks that go with it, and you won't have to go to the trouble of explaining them. Furthermore, people will feel comfortable with the things you say, because they are familiar with the metaphor; it's like a house they've lived in or a shoe they've worn, and they just *know* that you are someone they can follow with confidence. When John F. Kennedy organized the language of his presidency around the New Frontier, he knew this, and the effect was predictable. The message was approximately "Follow me, and once again, the bad guys will always lose, there will always be more of everything, women will never smell bad . . . " and so forth. He had no need to spell all that out. And even if your plan is nothing more complex than getting fifteen people to the same picnic on time, the unifying metaphor is the handiest and most charismatic way of doing it.

What you must watch out for, however, is a metaphor with presuppositions that hadn't occurred to you and won't help. For example, in California's 1976 election there was a proposal on the ballot to do something about the problem of smoking in public. According to all the polls and questionnaires, this proposal was in excellent shape, despite all the money of the tobacco industry that opposed it. Even smokers, according to the polls, would welcome a solution to the nuisance of being hassled to put out their cigarettes and being glared at by people in restaurants and all the rest of that. Logic was on the side of the proposal. Common sense was on the side of the proposal. The voters, it appeared, were on the side of the proposal. But the measure was resoundingly whipped at the polls all the same.

There were a number of reasons for this, but a major one was the unifying metaphor invoked by the slogan the proposal carried with it. It was "Clean Indoor Air."

Who could possibly be against clean indoor air? Everybody. As a unifying metaphor, CLEAN INDOOR AIR carries with it a list like this:

1. Nobody likes to clean house, but somebody has to do it, and it's probably you.
2. If there are rings around the shirt collars at your house, you're disgusting.
3. If there's a ring around the toilet bowl at your house, you're disgusting.
4. If your glassware doesn't shine and sparkle, you're stupid; don't you even know which detergent to use, dummy?
5. Air that is clean does not smell—have you changed your kitty litter, or not?
6. Air that is clean does not smell—have you run around the house spraying everything like a decent person would, or not?
7. If you don't keep the air clean inside your house, your family will be embarrassed, and nobody will want to come have coffee at your place, and you'll be unpopular.
   (and so on . . .)

That is, the decision was to choose between the Marlboro Man and the individual a friend of mine calls Tommy Tidy Bowl. Once this metaphor had been drummed into the minds of the voters, no amount of money could have saved that proposal.

When you choose a metaphor, be sure you know what its presuppositions are. In an emergency, just shout, "Wagons, ho!" and stand back out of the way; you'll be amazed at how effective that is all by itself. Everybody moves.

You cannot be charismatic with any of the following as your unifying metaphors: The Clean Little Cottage; The Good Little Boy; The Cheerful Factory. (At least a beginner can't; it is possible that millions of dollars and a few experts could.) More likely choices are these: The Proud Ship Sailing; Miss America; The Football Game. When you think of a good unifying metaphor, or when a commercial, an advertisement, or a speech makes you think of one, write it down; you may be able to use it later.

Culturally Loaded Vocabulary

The last of our charisma producers is closely related to the preceding one. Certain words and phrases are heavily loaded—either positively or negatively—within the cultural group that uses them. Small children learn at an amazingly early age that one sure way to get attention is to use one of the negative ones.

If you want to be perceived as charismatic, you need to know the culturally loaded vocabulary of the person(s) you are talking to, and whether their values are positive or negative. Certain items will trigger positive presuppositions, others will trigger negative ones, and you need to know which is which. Some of these are overpoweringly obvious. No subtle explanation is required to let you know that you must be careful with ethnic terms, curses, endearments, and current media clichés.

Within any group that is reasonably familiar to you your problems should be minor. You will know what items are on the list, whether their value is positive or negative, and when to use which ones. For dealing with persons from a group that is unfamiliar, you must do some advance research, preferably by discussing the matter with someone who is native to that group. (This is a topic for the expert, not the beginner, and won't be discussed in this book. It will be obvious to you that it can't be accomplished by simply sitting down with the informed individual and saying, "By the way, I need to know which words and phrases are taboo in your group, and which ones people really like to hear.")

A word that I have used frequently in this book—"Anglo"—will serve us well as an example. In the United States "Anglo" is an ethnic label roughly comparable to "Chicano" or "Latino" or "Black" or a number of others that come readily to mind. Certainly it qualifies as a culturally loaded term. But does it have a positive or a negative value in your speech?

That depends. If the group or person you are speaking to uses the set of terms including "Mexican American," "Afro American," "Native American," and "Asian American," the term "Anglo" is probably one with negative presuppositions attached. If the person would never breathe any of those words but would instead say things such as "you know who I mean" and "people who aren't like us," you can be absolutely certain that the word "Anglo" is as negative as a loaded cannon. The dialogue that follows demonstrates how not to be charismatic in this respect:

CONFRONTATION TWENTY-FIVE

Employer: I've called you in because I have a lot of respect for you, Bob, and I think your advice could be of help right now.

Employee: Well, I appreciate that. Anything I can do, anytime. What's the problem?

Employer: It's something that baffles me, frankly. I mean, it's made very clear around here how things are supposed to be run. There's a sign on the wall—it says any employee more than three minutes late reports to the supervisor immediately. That's *clear*, right?

Employee: Certainly.

Employer: And they *know*—all of them—that if they're late, they are going to get docked for it. They *know* that.

Employee: Yes, sir. That's correct.

Employer: Then will you please explain to me, Bob, just one thing: *Why* do they keep coming in late every day?

Employee: I think that's an easy one.

Employer: I knew I could count on you, Bob.

Employee: The problem, sir, is that we're Anglos and they're not.

(This did not start as a confrontation—but it ended as one.)

It's not that EMPLOYEE here should not point out to his boss that the difficulty lies in differing perceptions about time in different ethnic groups, if that is in fact what's causing the tardiness upsetting EMPLOYER. Not at all. The problem is the use of the word "Anglo." EMPLOYEE may perceive both himself and EMPLOYER as Anglos, but EMPLOYER obviously does *not;* and he will have no further interest in Bob's opinions. There are a number of reasonably safe ways to convey the same information without using a term that will trigger so much negative emotion. For example:

"The problem, sir, is that the Protestant Ethic is not really part of everyone's cultural heritage."

OR . . .

"Sir, different groups of people have different ways of looking at time. I think that's at the root of the difficulty."

One of these responses might allow EMPLOYER and EMPLOYEE to go on with the discussion and exchange some useful information. But the line "We're Anglos and they're not" can only be the end of all meaningful communication between these two.

This is clearly a tricky area once you are beyond the most simplistic examples. I will be giving more examples—and more complex ones—in the special chapters in this book specifically directed to college students, men, and women, respectively. But the basic principles should be clear.

If you are certain that a particular item has a positive value as culturally loaded vocabulary, *use* it if you can; this will set up a feeling that you are someone trustworthy. Avoid negatively loaded items. If you're not sure which value an item has, leave it out of your speech completely. If you find yourself in trouble, go to Computer Mode, use the most neutral and abstract vocabulary you can, and maintain that mode until you have more information to tell you what is appropriate.

REFERENCES AND SUGGESTED READINGS

Books:

ELGIN, SUZETTE H. *Pouring Down Words*. Englewood Cliffs, N.J.: Prentice-Hall, Inc., 1975. (Especially Chapter Six, "Political Language and Its Structure"; and Chapter Nine, "Language and the Media.")

GRINDER, JOHN, and RICHARD BANDLER. *Structure of Magic II*. Palo Alto, Calif.: Science and Behavior Books, Inc., pp. 3–26. (This book is devoted almost exclusively to techniques for therapy; however, the section cited discusses the language patterns associated with the various sensory modes.)

Articles:

EDELMAN, MURRAY. "Language, Myths and Rhetoric." *Society,* July–August 1976, pp. 14–21. (An excellent discussion of metaphor.)

GELDARD, FRANK A. "Body English." *Psychology Today,* December 1968, pp. 43–47. (This is a discussion of research on the sensory capabilities of the skin and the sense of touch.)

GOLEMAN, DANIEL. "People Who Read People." *Psychology Today,* July 1979, pp. 66–78. (This article describes the method of verbal training and analysis called Neurolinguistic Programming, developed by Grinder, Bandler, and their associates. It has much to say about charisma.)

HELLER, CELIA S. "Chicano Is Beautiful." *Commonweal,* January 23, 1970, pp. 454–458. (A language-centered article on Chicano, Black, and Anglo ethnic groups.)

KNIGHT, ARTHUR. "The Way of the Western: More Mire than Myth." *Saturday Review,* March 1973, p. 38.

LEONARD, GEORGE B. "Language and Reality." *Harper's,* November 1974, pp. 46–52. (This is an extensive discussion of the power of metaphor and language to shape our perceptions of reality. Highly recommended.)

NOVAK, MICHAEL. "White Ethnic." *Harper's,* September 1971, pp. 44–50. (This article takes up the discussion of groups such as the Irish, Polish, and other white ethnic populations in the United States. Highly recommended.)

WAX, ROSALIE, and ROBERT K. THOMAS. "American Indians and White People." *Phylon* (Atlanta University), Winter 1961, pp. 37–46. (This article is especially valuable for its detailed description of differences in nonverbal behavior between the two groups under discussion. Highly recommended.)

Verbal Interaction Power Networks

14

You are now equipped with a set of basic skills for verbal self-defense and should be ready to begin putting them to use in your everyday life. The questions that now come up are, when do you use your new skills, where do you use them, and to what extent?

Within any culture, or any subgroup of a culture, all language behavior is determined by rules. The fact that most of these rules are not part of the conscious awareness of those using them does not make them any less binding. It does lead to confusion, since there is a strong tendency to assume that some people just "have a knack" for communicating with others and that because it's all done on an intuitive basis there's nothing you can do but envy such people. (This is similar to the idea that people are "born with charisma.") You will now be well aware that this is not an accurate idea—for which we can all be thankful. There is a very concrete system for answering the questions at the end of the first paragraph in this chapter; you do not have to "play it by ear."

All human beings function in networks of interaction with others. Your family is such a network, the people with whom you work or study are another, your friends are a third (and may be several separate networks), and so on. How many networks you are involved in, how much they overlap and intermesh, will depend upon your personal life-style, but only if you live in total isolation from the world can you escape them. I doubt that such isolation can be achieved on this planet today.

Below is an illustration of one such network, called a

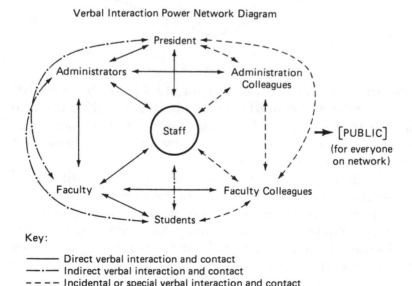

Verbal Interaction Power Network Diagram

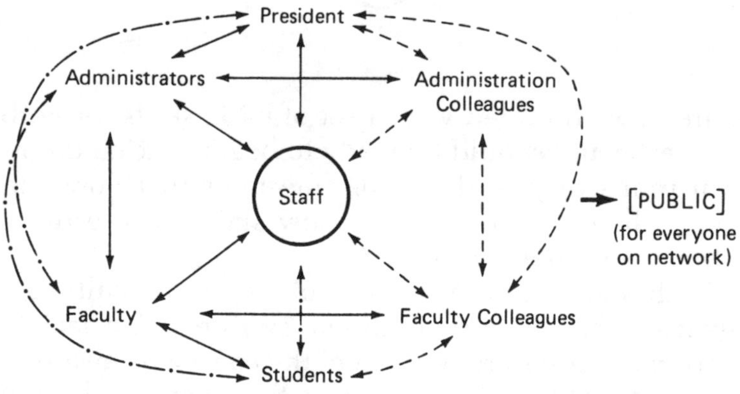

Key:

——— Direct verbal interaction and contact
—·— Indirect verbal interaction and contact
- - - - Incidental or special verbal interaction and contact

Verbal Interaction Power Network Diagram. Almost any group would serve equally well as an example, but I have chosen the academic environment of a large state college, because it is the one with which I am most familiar.

This diagram lays out for you the typical verbal interactions for this particular network. As you can see by using the key to the lines, a faculty member will ordinarily be in direct verbal contact with other members of the faculty, with the administration immediately above him or her in rank, with the students, and with the staff. There will be indirect contact with the president of the college at an occasional meeting or social event. An administrator, on the other hand, unless the position is one specifically requiring constant contact with students, will encounter them only indirectly.

The dotted lines represent special relationships, which will always be either utterly trivial or extremely important. Notice that the president is shown as in direct contact with individual administrators. However, the line from president to administration colleagues is a broken one. This means that although the president would be expected to be directly available to any administrator, it would be unusual for him or her to become involved in the internal interaction of one administrator with another. Similarly, although faculty are in direct contact with one another, it is not usual for them to become involved in the internal affairs of the administrators. The dotted lines ordinarily represent situations such as the following:

1. A member of the secretarial staff finds himself or herself caught in a feud between two administrators who are not speaking to each other and who use the staff member as a kind of messenger.
2. A student becomes entangled in a power struggle between two faculty members, both of whom want the student to emerge as their personal protégé.

3. A member of the administration is married to a faculty member and therefore becomes involved socially with a part of the network that would ordinarily only be in indirect contact with him or her.

These special situations cannot be anticipated, although you must be alert for them. They require careful handling, since the individual lowest in the power hierarchy is ordinarily the one to suffer if mistakes are made in the situation.

This diagram should remind you of those maps you find in public places with a little dot saying, "You Are Here." However, these networks, unlike maps of buildings, are not stable. The moment you place yourself on the diagram as the dot representing your own position, the entire map will change to reflect the way it looks from *your* point of view. The figure on page 236 is therefore a neutral and abstract representation, with many artificial features. For example, every group in the network appears to be equal in power relative to all the others—and that is certainly not accurate.

Furthermore, the diagram is drawn as if there were only one level for each group—again, this is not realistic. Each group on the network will have another network unique to *it*, with numerous levels that have their own interrelationships. Thus, although the president will be in direct contact with some levels of the staff—for instance, his or her own personal secretary—there will be hundreds of people working at the college that he may never so much as see during his entire career there. The president may be in direct contact with some levels of the administration but may almost never encounter the assistant deans. Students will be in constant and maddening direct contact with the staff in the offices to which they must go for grade records, petitions, admissions forms, and so on, but they are unlikely ever to have anything to do with the personal secretary to the vice-president for academic affairs.

And because a state college is supported by public funds and is a part of the real world, everyone on the network has a relationship of some kind with that nebulous entity, the Public.

Now, how do you go about using the diagram concept as a guide for your use of verbal self-defense skills?

First, decide on a reasonably uncomplicated network of which you are a part, one that you know well, and draw a diagram for it like the one on page 236. It should be a neutral diagram, with the same artificial characteristics as the example. Decide which interactions in the network are direct, which are indirect, and which are incidental; decide whether all of them are two-way relationships that should have an arrow at both ends. (Because it is surprisingly difficult to decide these things, you may want to choose a small network for your first attempt at this.)

Second, when you are sure that you have made your diagram as accurate as possible, draw a new diagram for the same network, but this time put yourself in the center of the diagram. The "You Are Here" position, for any network you function in, will always be central, in the spot where "Staff" was placed in the figure on page 236. Now redraw the rest of the diagram to indicate the way power relationships and verbal interactions are represented from your position at the center. You will then have a diagram that is accurate for you personally within that network, rather than an artificial diagram that has only an abstract connection with your life.

For each network that is an important part of your life, you should go through at least the second step of this process. Only the first pair should be difficult, and you need the full set. Furthermore, anytime that you add a new network to your life—for example, if you change jobs or graduate from college—you should prepare a new set of diagrams reflecting the changes.

Can you do all this in your head instead of going through the tedious process of putting it all on paper? Perhaps. If you're able to do that, and feel confident that way, fine. At first, however, there is a strong probability that you will overlook or distort an important interaction relationship. I strongly recommend taking the time and making the effort to get all your information laid out neatly before you where you can refer to it as your own situation changes. Remember that these are fluid maps; unless you are convinced that your relationships will never change in any way, they are a useful device for keeping track of shifts in status or power that affect you directly. And although you may be determined that there shall be no change in your life, others may take that decision out of your hands, often with little warning.

Now let's return to the illustration on page 236 and see how you would work with it if it were a primary network in your own life. Since the example is drawn with "Staff" at center position, we'll discuss it from that point of view.

Assume that you have just been hired for a position as administrative assistant to an assistant dean in the School of Sciences. (Administrative assistant is a semiclerical position, much like that of an executive secretary but with more responsibility and with greater prestige in the academic network.) Look at the following scenarios and consider what changes you might want to make in the way the diagram is drawn:

1. There are four other assistant deans, each with an administrative assistant like yourself. Above you are two associate deans, as well as *the* dean. Your college has six divisions like the School of Sciences, each with an administrative structure roughly comparable to yours. Then, beyond those

six deans, there is a level of administration with four assistant vice-presidents, two associate vice-presidents, three vice-presidents of one thing or another, and—finally—the college president. What changes do you make?

ANSWER: The line from "Staff" to "President" should become a broken one indicating only indirect interaction. Your chances of having to interact verbally with the president, given all that hierarchy between the two of you, are very slim.

2. There are two other assistant deans, but neither of them has an administrative assistant. The other two have a personal secretary instead. There is one associate dean, the dean proper, and beyond that there is the same structure described in Scenario A. Your college has six divisions like the School of Sciences, each with a few assistant deans, no more than two associate deans, and a dean at the head. Only one other assistant dean in the entire college has an administrative assistant. What changes do you make?

ANSWER: The line from "Staff" to "President" becomes a broken line, as in Scenario 1. However, things are not quite the same. The fact that your boss is one of only two people at his or her rank with an administrative assistant probably means that he or she is headed for an associate deanship, either increasing the number of associate deans in the School of Sciences or replacing the present one. Since you have no way of knowing which of these two alternatives is likely, you need a special direct line to the personal staff of the present associate dean. If your boss is going to be replacing their boss, you need a way to get an early warning on that, as well as a firm relationship between you and that group to serve as a base for the sudden interaction that you'll have to handle when the replacement happens. The line you are drawing is hypothetical at this point—it will be up to you to use your verbal self-defense skills to make it a real one.

If you compare the two hypothetical scenarios, you will see how the diagrams are used and why they matter. In the first example, you could ask yourself whether you need to worry about verbal interaction with the president of the college, and the answer would be no. Unless some unusual situation (dotted-line variety) developed, you could be sure that use of your new skills relative to the president would be a waste of time and energy, leading nowhere. (This also holds for the second example.) In Scenario 1, so far as you can tell at this stage of the game, all administrators at the rank your boss holds are on a roughly equal level, [and you are one among others who hold an equal rank of staff.] You should expect to need to put your energies into direct verbal interaction with your boss and the other administrative assistants, and indirectly with the dean and associate dean. The situation appears to be in balance.

Scenario 2 is quite different. The power relationships are changing in some way that you, as a new staff member, will need to keep an eye on. You can anticipate that whether your boss becomes another associate dean or replaces the present one, there will be verbal confrontations with much tension ahead of you, and you are going to be part of them. You need to find out some things, and the best way to do that is by using your verbal self-defense skills. For example:

1. Do the personal secretaries of the other two assistant deans resent your being hired as administrative assistant to your boss? This is likely—though not inevitable—because one potential applicant for the job you've just filled could have been one of *them*. They may feel that you have been brought in over their heads, unfairly. You need to find out whether they applied for the job you got, and if so, why they failed to get it instead of you. This matters very much, since you must work with them.

2. Is there already tension between the present associate dean, and his or her staff, and your boss? (There may not be. It is at this level that, in accordance with the Peter Principle, you tend to find people who seem to have no sense at all of what is going on around them in terms of interaction.) Even if the administrator seems to be oblivious to the coming upheaval, the staff will probably be well aware of it. You'll need to check both parts of the question separately.

3. Are there any bodies buried anywhere? This is one of those dotted-line matters. That is, are there private feuds or private friendships at levels that would not be predictable from the diagram? If so, you need to know about them and put a warning line on your diagram indicating that the persons involved are possible sources of conflict and are to be treated with every bit of skill you have in *any* verbal interaction.

What you are doing is deciding, based on information that you now have and to which you will keep adding as you continue in your work, *who* are possible sources of verbal confrontation and therefore require your attention, who can safely be eliminated from that set unless the situation changes drastically, who are individuals that you may deal with in a relaxed manner, and so on. That is—when, where, and to what extent do you use your verbal self-defense skills in this network?

It's foolish to waste your time trying complicated maneuvers with an administrator who has gone as far as he or she will ever go in the college, who is completely powerless to do you either good or harm in your career or in your personal life, and who has been, from the point of view of the rest of the network, "retired" from the power chain to a permanent holding position.

A caution here: I am *not*, most emphatically not,

saying that you should treat this individual with anything but the utmost courtesy and respect. Remember that we are talking about self-defense, not attacks. But the colleges are full of ludicrous examples of staff wasting valuable time trying to build strong relationships with administrators of this kind because they do not realize that they are at a dead end. You have only so much time and energy to spread around, and your job network is not the only one you must deal with. Don't *waste* your energies. In this same category you should put being afraid of people who cannot possibly harm you, which creates unnecessary tension and disrupts the entire network not only for you but for many people who must interact with you.

If your job matters to you, if you want to be successful in it without the job becoming an obsession that has serious negative effects on your health and your personal life, you must know what the power structure is like. You must know where you fit into it, what measures are required of you in terms of personal interaction, and how to go about carrying out those measures. You *must* have what is called a "support structure," and the only way you will get one is by building it. It will not build itself.

Nasty moral time.

It ought to be true that the support structure and the job success would come of themselves, automatically, as a result of your being a good person who does your work properly. I am sorry to have to tell you that the game is not played that way. People who assume it is will be trampled upon and will usually never know what hit them. Your decision, the one that matters, is whether you intend to deal with this unpleasant truth offensively or defensively. If your choice is an offensive strategy, the shelves are full of manuals on how to fight your way to the top over the bleeding bodies of those you knife. You'll have no trouble finding these books; most are best sellers. This book, on the other hand, is intended to prepare you for the defensive choice, and to equip you to deal with the consequences of having made it.

Your support structure is crucial. There must be people you can count on, whether you are around or not. There have to be people who, hearing a rumor about you, will be willing to come to your defense. (If you do your job well, there will be rumors; they are a by-product of jealousy.) They also have to be people who will then come to you to find out the truth of the matter, so that you know what is going on—or who know when that is not appropriate. Without such a structure you are at the mercy of many fish with big teeth working their way upstream.

The strategies outlined above, and all the steps within them, can be applied to every network you find yourself in. Your household should be analyzed this way, with scrupulous care; you may be astonished at the sources of tension you will find and that you had not realized were there. Your job, your friends, your health network, *any* set of interpersonal contacts that you must deal with using oral rather than written language, should be approached in the same way that the academic network was analyzed in this chapter. Then add your other techniques and use them to keep the networks working, stable, and in a positive equilibrium as part of your life.

SUGGESTED READINGS

Book:

TOFFLER, ALVIN. *Future Shock.* New York: Bantam Books, Inc., 1972. Chapters Six and Seven, pp. 95–142. (This is, in my opinion, the best basic source available on personal interaction in the rapidly changing framework of today's society. Highly recommended.)

Articles:

DELLINGER, R. W. "Keeping Tabs on the Joneses." *Human Behavior,* November 1977, pp. 22–30. (An article on the subject of status, how it is demonstrated, and how its indicators are changing today.)

HARRAGAN, BETTY L. "Why Corporations Are Teaching Men to Think Like Women: And Other Secret Game Plans That You May Not Have Been Briefed On." *Ms. Magazine,* June 1977, pp. 62–63 and 87–88.

LAMOTT, KENNETH. "The Money Revolution." *Human Behavior,* April 1978, pp. 18–23. (This brief article discusses the changing attitudes in America toward getting ahead. It should provide you with an idea of some of the offensive strategies for interaction.)

YANKELOVICH, DANIEL. "Who Gets Ahead in America." *Psychology Today,* July 1979, pp. 28–43 and 90–91.

Special Chapter

College Students

15

As college students, you have special problems in verbal self-defense that are not typical of any other population group and which create for you situations that—if they appeared in a work of fiction—would be rejected as "too unbelievable." I can vouch for the truth of this; I spent twelve years as a college student myself, and have been teaching college students ever since, and those unbelievable things do happen. Absolutely.

Your situation will differ depending on whether you attend a small private school or a huge open-admissions state university; whether you are a graduate or an undergraduate; whether you are returning to school after years in the armed services (or business or as a homemaker or parent) or are going straight on to college from high school; whether you must go to school and work and try to take care of a home as well or are free to devote all your time to your academic responsibilities; and whether some special qualification, such as a physical disability or having a native language other than English applies to you. I cannot in this single chapter cover all these eventualities, and I am going to try to speak to a hypothetical "average" student. No such creature exists, of course, but we'll make do.

I will try to discuss aspects of verbal self-defense that would be useful for the widest possible range of students. But I want to begin by stating that the first step should be one I have already discussed in detail, in Chapter Fourteen. Only you have the necessary information to draw a Verbal Power Interaction Network that represents your own academic situation from your own point of view. You should do that at once. If you are a handicapped student, the Disabled Student Services staff (or their equivalent on your campus) will have a place on that diagram. If you are a veteran, the Veterans Affairs Office will play a part in your life. If you work on campus, you have a different relationship with both faculty and staff than do the other students. If you attend an exclusive and expensive residential school, there are special circumstances that will show up on your diagram—sit down and make them clear. If you live in a dormitory, the diagram must show your relationships in the dorm; if you live off-campus, the network will show the members of your household and, if you rent your housing, the individual you rent from. By using the Network Diagram you can clarify your situation for yourself, no matter how different it may be from that of the mythical "average student" I am speaking to. Begin with that step.

Next I am going to go once more around the Verbal Violence Octagon, specifically for the student, giving examples from each section. These utterances are examples that should immediately alert you to the possibility of a confrontation. If you feel that you would be confused by any one of them or uncertain about how to handle it, you should go back and review the chapter in this book that deals with that section of the Octagon.

- *Section A:* "If you *really* wanted to pass this course, you'd write a term paper."

  "If you *really* wanted to be accepted at this school, you wouldn't dress like that."

  "If you *really* wanted to get into this department, you'd retake the entrance exams."
- *Section B:* "If you *really* wanted to graduate, you wouldn't be *interested* in going to parties."

  "If you *really* cared about getting a loan, you wouldn't *want* to walk in here looking like a bum."

  "If you *really* wanted to join this sorority/fraternity, you wouldn't *want* to spend so much time with that Frasier person."
- *Section C:* "Don't you even *care* what your grade point average is going to be?"

  "Don't you even *care* whether you get into a decent graduate school or not?"

  "Don't you even *care* that other students in this class must sit and wait while I answer your continual questions?"
- *Section D:* "Even an *undergraduate* should be thoroughly familiar with every word in the official catalog of this institution."

"Even a *chemistry* major should have *some* idea who Rimbaud was."

"Even a student with problems like *yours* ought to know at least the basic elements of English grammar."

- *Section E:* "Everyone understands why you are having a hard time keeping your grades up to the minimum level at this school."

  "Everyone in this class understands perfectly why you feel obligated to disrupt every class meeting with foolish behavior."

  "Everyone understands why you always feel forced to display your brilliance and make all the other students feel inferior."

- *Section F:* "A student who really *wanted* to do well in life would have better sense than to choose a dead-end major like you did."

  "A student who is just not properly prepared to do college work really can't expect to pass at a good school like this one."

  "A student whose outside obligations come before academic work really has no place in college, I'm afraid."

- *Section G:* "Why don't you try—just *once*—to get your work in on time?"

  "Why don't you behave like other students for a change and see what happens?"

  "Why is it that every time I look up from this desk, you are standing there waiting for me to make some special arrangement on your behalf? Don't you *ever* think of anybody but yourself?"

- *Section H:* "*Some* instructors would find it very difficult to believe that anyone who has almost

> no grasp of the basics could have the gall to enroll in Advanced Composition."
>
> "*Some* people in our class might think it was pretty strange if they saw a student shut himself up in the prof's office for hours at a time."
>
> "*Some* parents would make a real production out of it if they spent thirty-five hundred dollars a year putting a kid through school and couldn't even count on that kid's holding a C average."

Remember, when you are trying to decide whether utterances that come at you are attacks or sincere (though perhaps unwelcome) efforts to help, listen for the *stresses*. Identify the speaker's Satir Mode. And work out the presuppositions of the utterances. If you aren't facing an attack, don't respond defensively. If you are, and you come out of it badly, write down what happened in your Journal and work through it—what did you do wrong? Sometimes the answer will be "Nothing." Sometimes you will simply be up against greater experience, greater knowledge or sophistication, or greater force, and you will lose in spite of having done just what you should. But at least know what happened, and learn from it. If the person who trounced you is one you're going to have to encounter a lot while you're at college, put a warning symbol beside him or her on your network diagram to remind you that this one means trouble. Then you will be wary when you approach that individual again.

Liars, especially, should be circled in red or marked with an X or whatever identifying device you prefer. For example, instructors who say there will be no final and then give one, staff who tell you that you have filled out a form properly and then not only bounce it back at you but charge you a late fee for doing it "right" the second time, students who borrow your notes or your books with a promise to return them and then don't. Such people are liars, and they are to be found on every campus. Getting taken in by them over and over again because they are *charismatic* liars or because you can't be bothered to keep track of who they are is a foolish way to go through college. (If you find the term "unreliable people" less abrasive than "liars," use that. Just identify them.)

And while we're on the subject, be sure you identify the "Good Guys" as well, whatever their sex. (A generally reliable source of information on all these matters is other students, when they agree in large numbers. Don't take the word of one or two individuals, who may have turned a single experience into a general pattern in their imaginations.) It's important to know which instructors can be counted on to play fair, which staff members really will look over the forms you turn in carefully to be sure they're properly done, and so on. This is valuable information.

Now I have twelve rules—very basic and elementary rules—for you to use in your verbal interactions with faculty members, at any level. They are as follows:

RULE 1

Be *sure* that the instructor knows what name is attached to your face, and vice versa. You may think that is automatic, but it isn't; and it's crucial. When the instructor is filling in final grades, and Student X has a point total that puts him or her right on the border line between a C and a B, a decision has to be made: Is there any reason to give this student an extra point or two and bump the grade up to a B? If the instructor can't even remember who Student X is, which is not at all unlikely if he or she teaches one hundred or more students every term, no such reason will come to mind. It may not be fair, but it's human, like the instructor.

Make a point, therefore, of going to the instructor's office at least once during the term, during regular office hours, and introducing yourself. Have a reasonable question to ask if possible; if you can't think of anything, just Level. Say: "I'm here to introduce myself." Be sure that you are recognized and will be remembered.

Obviously, if you are the class superstar, this rule does not apply to you, and you needn't take up the instructor's time. It is one of the great unsolved enigmas of academic life that it is almost always the straight-A student who does drop by—usually to ask if he or she ought to do an extra-credit project.

RULE 2

Eliminate, forever and ever, from your verbal behavior the mannerism linguists call *Hedging.* Typical Hedges are

- "I know this is probably a stupid question, but . . . "
- "I'm sure everybody else knows the answer to this question except me, but . . . "
- "I know I'm wasting your time asking this question, but . . . "
- "I know this is against the rules and there's no point in even asking for an exception, but . . . "
- "I know you said we couldn't turn in our papers late, but . . . "

- "I know you probably already told us this, but . . ." (and so on . . .)

These utterances are exactly equivalent to wearing a big sign that says, "Please kick me—I would love to be a victim." Get rid of them.

RULE 3

Never use any verbal mode or pattern with an instructor that carries the message "Okay, we're equals. No need to make any concessions for me, because I can do anything you can." Unless an instructor is a verbal bully, he or she will have a rule that says you don't humiliate students in front of other people or make fools of them in ways that will fester and hurt. This rule is from the "Pick on People Your Own Size" Popular Wisdom collection. If you suspend this rule by making it absolutely clear to the instructor that, so far as you're concerned, you two *are* the same size (or you're bigger), then anything goes. And the chances of you winning the resulting encounters are about one in one hundred thousand. The instructor has all the power, and you cannot win this one, whether you are right or not.

If you break this rule, of course, you can forget about Rule 1 for the instructor in question—you *will* be remembered. Some students try to wiggle their way around this rule with Hedges. That is, they say, "I know you're the one with the Ph.D. in here, and I'm probably crazy to say what I'm going to say, but I'm sure that what you told us is not the generally accepted position on that matter in the discipline." Never use Hedges, period. And please notice the strangeness of that utterance—it Placates all the way up to "but I'm sure" and then moves into a vocabulary and style associated only with academic discourse at an advanced level. This is well on its way to Distracter Mode.

RULE 4

Remember that if you accepted an arrangement of some kind in a class or office session and did not protest it, you are stuck with it. If you sat through the opening six weeks and never once asked what the grade would be based on, and it is announced in the seventh week that it's based on a final exam and four term papers and two oral presentations, *learn* from that. It is the faculty member's obligation to make clear what is expected of you very early in the course. If that obligation is not fulfilled and everybody just sits there, then it is assumed that you have all agreed to that arrangement. Complaining won't help; the instructor will add two more papers and a field trip, and you have not one toe to stand on. The time to raise objections to course requirements is in the first week, preferably in office hours—if you don't know what the requirements (or the office hours) are, you can't do this very effectively.

RULE 5

When you want a faculty member to do something for you—take you on for an independent study course, write you a letter of recommendation, etc.—take with you everything you can prepare in advance and be ready to present it. If it's a letter you want written, have all the information needed, an addressed envelope with a stamp on it, and anything else that might be useful. The fact that you tried to make it convenient is what counts, even if you have made a mistake and it has to be redone. *Never* try any of the following:

- "I want to do an independent study with you, and I came to see if you had any good ideas for one."
- "I want to do a term paper for extra credit, and I came by to see if you could suggest a good topic."
- "I know our papers are due tomorrow, so I thought I'd better come by and ask you for a couple of topics I could write on."
- "You don't remember me, but I had a class from you three years ago, and I can't find anybody else to ask for a letter of recommendation."

Students do these things—frequently—and thereby win themselves permanent exemptions from Rule 1. In justice to the helpless student who really and truly cannot think of a topic for the paper or the study and is not the sort of idiot he or she will be taken for if one of the sentences just listed is used to convey that message, here's what you *should* do. Go in and suggest a topic that you know the instructor will reject—that should be easy. The instructor will then make an alternative suggestion, and you have not made a fool of yourself. As with the response to the Section G attack, there is always the remote possibility that your anthropology professor will leap at the chance to do an independent study project with you on French milk jugs in the Middle Ages, and if that happens, you had better go ahead and do it. You are still better off than you were with no topic—and you haven't broken any of the rules.

RULE 6

If you behave like a doormat, expect to be stepped on and don't complain about it. Placating will get you stepped on.

For example:

Instructor: How many pages of reading a week do you think would be reasonable for your project, Miss Z?

Student: Oh, I don't know anything about that! You're the expert! Whatever you say is fine with me!

Instructor: I think one hundred pages a week should about cover it, then.

If this happens to you, remember—you asked for it.

RULE 7

Before you alienate a faculty member for a *stupid* reason—such as how good it would make you feel to demonstrate to the entire class what an idiot he or she is—remember this: The day is almost certain to arrive when you need to ask that instructor for something. A letter of recommendation. A job. An incomplete grade. Permission to take an exam late. Something like that. When that day comes, the answer will probably be no.

I am not talking here about alienating instructors for good and sufficient reasons. There *are* some—matters of principle for which the consequences are a risk you take as an ethical position. They are very different; there's nothing ethical about humiliating someone in public.

RULE 8

Never let an instructor find out that you have not read whatever it was that you were supposed to read, unless you've been asked directly and would have to lie to conceal that fact. (If you let yourself be manipulated into a corner like that, you need to review your verbal self-defense skills and find out where the opening is.) This goes for the description of the course in the catalog, the class syllabus and the sheet of course requirements, the dittoed reading list, and so on, just as much as it does for the assigned reading. Ask a question *about* the item you haven't read; ask for clarification, explaining that you're not sure you understand; but for heaven's sake, if you failed to read something and are in trouble as a result, don't mention it.

RULE 9

If you aren't sure whether you were ever given anything to read about some basic information item for the course or can't remember whether the instructor ever said anything about it in class, do not ask the instructor. Ask another student, preferably the superstar mentioned previously. It is unutterably absurd to go down in history in your instructor's memory as the student who, on the next to last day of the term, raised a hand and asked, "Is there a final exam in this class?"

RULE 10

Never argue with an instructor in front of other students or other faculty or other *anybody.* (The only exception is the rare case in which it really is a matter of principle.) Let's assume that the instructor *has* made a mistake, and knows it; and that you have challenged him or her in front of the entire class, and you are right. You have now created a classic Cornered Carnivore Scene, and if you are eaten alive do not expect sympathy. There is no way on earth to predict what a faculty member in this kind of trap will do, and some of the possibilities are more than bizarre.

What do you do about your obligation to be sure that the rest of the students share your correct information instead of the instructor's misconceptions? This is an ideal opportunity to apply Rule 1; drop by the instructor's office and discuss the disputed information. You say, "You know, I read an article the other day that completely contradicted what you said to us this morning about the Beetlehopper Hypothesis, and now I'm confused. If you'd discuss it with me for a few minutes, I'd appreciate it." The two of you are now alone, the instructor can admit the error if there is one and will usually pass the correction on to the rest of the class. (Properly, you should be credited when this happens; but if you aren't, the kind of nonverbal behavior necessary to get across to the class that you knew it all along is not appropriate. If it matters to you, you can always brag about it later—not in class.)

You will miss the glory of the big in-class duel, but the situation will have been taken care of with no loss of dignity to anyone. If this doesn't work, and the instructor persists in teaching what you know to be false information . . . that is what counselors are for. Go talk it over with one.

RULE 11

If you are a female student, do not ever present as an excuse for anything or a reason for asking for anything any of the following: (a) your menstrual period, your menopause, or your hysterectomy; (b) your pregnancy or your childbirth; (c) having been up all night with a new baby for any number of nights; (d) all your children having come down with the mumps, intestinal flu, and so forth. If you are a female student, I don't expect you to like this one little bit. If a male student asks for an extension on a paper because he has had an appendectomy, he will probably get it. This rule is one of those things that is so incredibly unfair that it defies description. Nevertheless, please remember what you are up against—two items from the Popular Wisdom chest: (a) women don't do well in school because of their "female" problems; and (b) women with children should not try to go to school because they won't be able to cope with both the schoolwork and their maternal duties. Every time you present one of the excuses on that list, you are reinforcing these two ideas, and you are doing no female student—yourself included—any favors. (If you are a *male* student who has been up with a baby for four nights in a row, you are probably safe with that excuse; it is perceived very differently.) My personal advice, with which many people would undoubtedly disagree, is that you should grit your teeth and bear it. The stereotype of the female student who enrolls year after year and always gives up in the first few weeks because she simply can't manage one of these "female problems" and academic work as well is a Unifying Metaphor that needs to be destroyed.

RULE 12

Sometimes, in spite of all your best intentions, you find yourself in a situation where you have *really* fouled it up. You are 100 percent in the wrong, you have no excuse for what you've done, and disaster approaches. Let us say, for example, that you enrolled in a class, went to it three or four times, did none of the work, forgot to drop it before the deadline, and are going to flunk. Or let's say that you challenged an instructor on some information and got nowhere trying to convince him or her that you were right; then you talked to a counselor, who got nowhere trying to convince you that you were wrong; next you spent quite a lot of time doing your duty to the other students in the class by telling them individually that the instructor is completely confused; and now, much too late, you have discovered that it is *you* who are in error. Either of these will do as a standard example of impending academic doom.

In such a case, there's only one thing you can do, and you're not going to like it. Go to the instructor's office hour, sit down, and Level. Say that you are there because you've done whatever ridiculous thing you have done, that you already know you have no excuse for it, and that you have come in to clear it up as best you can. Do not rationalize; do not talk about how this would never have happened if it hadn't been for some other instructor's behavior; do not mention something the instructor you are talking to should have done to ward this off; do not, in other words, try to spread your guilt around. Level and be done with it.

Be certain you aren't Placating, now! There's a big difference between a Leveler's "What I did was stupid, and I'm sorry I did it, and that's why I'm here" and the Placater's "I know you won't have any respect for me ever again after the awful, terrible thing I did, and I don't blame you one bit, and I'm so ashamed that I'd go kill myself except I'm so stupid I'd probably do *that* wrong, too, and if you threw me right out of there this minute, it would serve me right." *Please* don't do that last routine; it's nauseating.

When you go in and Level about your mistake, any number of things may happen, and you'll have to deal with them on an individual basis. Again, that's why colleges have counselers and ombudsmen and deans of students and advising centers. They are there to try to help you when you are in over your head. But *first,* you have to follow Rule 12 and see what happens. Given a decent set of odds, you'll be able to handle the consequences yourself; if not, it's time for an expert. Any other strategy, however, is certain only to make things worse.

It may help, as you look over these twelve rules, for you to remember a few things that tend to be lost in the academic shuffle. One is that the whole situation is artificial. You are an adult, probably an adult with adult responsibilities, often an adult accustomed to giving the orders and having them obeyed in at least one situation in your life. At college you are suddenly in the position of a child again in many ways, subject to the sort of sudden whims and irrational incomprehensibilities you associated with grown-ups when you were chronologically a child. I do not intend to try to explain to you what lies behind the absurdities you must deal with, most of which will be blamed upon "computer error." It would require a separate book. But keep firmly in mind that your situation, like childhood, is *temporary.* You will not be here, in what may seem to you not a temple of learning but a vast mental hospital, for more than a specific number of years, determined by your educational goal and your skill with the catalog. Say to yourself sternly, on the day when you are told that the twelve units of French which you were last year solemnly assured would allow you to graduate are no longer enough—you need three more units—and that whoever told you that twelve would do must have obtained that information from a bulletin that contained several "computer" errors: "This, too, shall pass. I do not have a life sentence at this place; I will be able to leave here and go on to other things."

If that doesn't do it, try shock therapy. Choose any incredible disaster that does *not* apply to you, and say to yourself, sternly, "I could have a *real* problem. I could have an incurable fatal disease. I could be on Death Row awaiting execution." Something of that kind. The point of this is to restore your sense of perspective, so that you do not have a nervous breakdown or assault an evaluations clerk over three units of French.

You must also remember that you are *normal.* That is, although the life of a college student may have been represented to you as a glorious series of wondrous events, the honest truth is that it rarely is that way. If it is true for you, be grateful. You are singularly blessed. Ordinarily only students in midstream—about halfway along toward their goal—have this kind of blessing vouchsafed them. For the student who has just started and therefore knows nothing at all about most things; for the student who is nearing the end of the academic trek and therefore nearing the day when all the accumulated "computer" and other errors will suddenly loom up cumulatively like Mount Everest; for either of those types of student, the following situation is normal.

You are exhausted; you are nervous; you are under stress; you have headaches and colds and rashes and stomach upsets; you have no confidence in yourself; you have no idea what ever made you start this process, and you are *certain* that whatever it was, you were out of your mind; and in any case, you are out of your mind. If you can accept the fact that this is the typical internal state of the college student, and if you are not in need of professional help, most of that list will melt away. You will look around you, you will talk to other students, you will ask faculty members young enough to remember being students, and you will find that there is nothing unique about your state. Everybody either feels that way, or did feel that way, as a student. And everybody did make it through college, go on to become a real person, turned out to be sane, stopped having colds and rashes and headaches and stomach upsets, and so on. *Talk* to a few people instead of listening only to your own internal repeating tape. And if indeed you do need professional help, if finding out that you are one of a vast crowd of people in your state of mind and body doesn't help, go get that professional help at once.

Finally, there is a mysterious phenomenon that will serve to finish off this chapter. I can only warn you about it, in the hope that foreknowledge will help you deal with it when you must. It applies primarily to graduate students, or students in intensive preprofessional programs such as prelaw, premedicine, and the like. For some reasons that I cannot hope to explain here, professors in these programs have usually developed a technique that is as insidious and subtle as time-release arsenic capsules. Some of them know they are doing it and are proud of it; others don't. Some do it because they consider it their duty to their students; others do it because their profs did it to them; others do it for no discernible reason. Whatever the motivation, the effect on the student is the same, and it goes like this:

> If you don't get an A in every course you take; if you don't get an A on every paper you write; if you don't win every prize and fellowship you apply for; if everything you submit for publication is not accepted (and so on); unless, to make it short, you are able to walk on water, you will feel an incredible burden of guilt. You feel that you have *failed your professor and let him or her down.* If you are enjoying yourself, no matter what you are doing or where you may be at the time, along comes the same burden of guilt—you should *not* be enjoying yourself. If you were living up to what you owe your professor, you would be reading the professional literature or writing a paper or giving a talk. At this point, you cease to enjoy yourself and might just as well give up and go write a paper, read something, reread something you've already read . . . anything to relieve the guilt.

This state is achieved by verbal manipulation, on all channels, and is widely alleged to do the student good "in the long run." Someday, in a book on *advanced* verbal self-defense, I will take the opportunity to explain how to escape it. But here and now, I can only let you know that it exists, that unless you are extremely lucky, it will have to be faced someday, and that the better prepared you are in the skills of verbal self-defense, the better your chances are of knowing what to do when that day comes.

SUGGESTED READINGS

Books:

GREER, COLIN. *The Great School Legend.* New York: The Viking Press, 1972. (This is a well-documented analysis of a number of myths and misconceptions about American education. Highly recommended.)

TOFFLER, ALVIN. *Future Shock.* New York: Bantam Books, Inc., 1972, pp. 398–427. (This chapter, called "Education in the Future Tense," discusses some of the changes that appear to be necessary if the academic system is to keep up with the real world.)

Articles:

FEDER, BERNARD. "How to Pass Without Actually Cheating." *Human Behavior,* June 1977, pp. 56–59.

MOLL, RICHARD W. "The College Admissions Game." *Harper's,* March 1978, pp. 24–30.

Special Chapter

For Men

16

It is my experience that only two types of men come to talk to me about verbal self-defense (usually after attending one of my workshops or seminars by mistake, under the impression that it was on some topic such as making a fortune in real estate).

The first type, and by far the most common, is the male who drops in specifically to inform me how very wrong I am. It may be, he tells me, that there are a handful of males in this country who are given to verbal bullying; after all, there are one or two rotten apples in any barrel. However, he tells me, such creatures are *rare.* (And, he adds, that's surprising, considering what they have to put up with.) The last thing he wants to tell me, as he leaves, is that above all I must know that *he* has never in his entire life carried out an act of verbal abuse, nor does he ever intend to. "And," he asks me, "don't you even *care* about the terrible effect of this nonsense you're telling people?" Exit, grim of face, duty done. (I have reached an age that prevents him from pointing out that I shouldn't worry my pretty little head about these things, or from patting me on said head as he goes by. Thank goodness.)

The second type is the male who arrives almost distraught, to tell me that for the first time in his life he realizes that he is a verbal bully, that he does it all the time, that he is perhaps raising his son to be a verbal bully, too, and what the devil is he supposed to do now that I've ruined his life? Sometimes he exits and sometimes he stays; and if he stays, we talk about it in roughly the way this chapter will read.

If Type I Male is absolutely sincere in what he says to me, he has no new problems. He is a confident and aggressive male, going about his business as usual. If he is *not* sincere but is trying hard to convince himself, then he has several new problems. One is the remolding of the little portion of his self-image that has been jerked about, so that it functions as it did before—confidently. Depending on how intelligent he is and what his principles are, this will vary in the amount of time and energy it requires. I do believe that the most common resolution is about a five-minute self-dialogue such as this one:

> "Could I possibly be a verbal bully? Me? Me, the guy who always remembers his mother's birthday? Me, the guy who *always* goes to that school play the kids are in, no matter how stupid it is? Me, the guy that never opens his mouth, no matter how many dumb things the other guys on the team do to wreck our chances for the season? Me, the guy

that everybody knows you can count on in any crisis? *Me?* Naaah. Impossible."

Any number of aunts, grandmothers, fathers, neighbors, pets, housemothers, friends, houseplants, or whatever you like, can be fit in there, as appropriate . . . and it's over forever. If it takes a little longer, he may have to put in some time keeping the walls up around the image for a while. For example, if he suddenly hears himself saying, "If you *really* wanted to . . . " and gets an odd feeling that that ought to mean something to him, he'll have to lay on more mortar fast. And he will have to deal with the minor burden of having engaged in self-doubt, however briefly, and explain to himself how he could have fallen for anything so trivial.

Type II Male has a larger problem. If he is now aware that he is a verbal abuser, he has to make a choice—to go on that way, knowing it, and live with what that means in his life, or to change it, which he suspects may be even worse than the first alternative. There is his self-image to be considered, you see, and his very real worry that if he changes it, he will somehow be less a man. "Gentleman" is one thing in his vocabulary; "gentle man" may be quite another. And then there is the burden of guilt. All his life he's been doing these things without realizing it—or did he maybe realize it all along and was enjoying it?—and he can't undo any of it. It's done. Over.

At the end of both this chapter and the chapter for women that follows, I have listed as a suggested reading an article by Susan Sontag called "The Double Standard of Aging." Usually, where these readings are concerned, I really am only suggesting that you go to them if they happen to interest you. This one, however, is the clearest and most compelling description I have ever read of the problems of both masculine and feminine self-image in

America and of what the threat to that self-image can mean for both sexes. Do not let its title mislead you. If you are a man, you need to know what it says about men—and perhaps, even more, what it says about women. (If you are a woman, the same thing is true, in reverse.) This one suggestion, then, falls into that class of things usually phrased like this: "You are *strongly urged* to read the article, as a supplement to the chapter."

From a man's point of view there seem to be two basic problems with the art of verbal self-defense. First, are you a verbal aggressor, even a verbal bully, or aren't you? How can you tell? Second, if the answer to the first question is yes, what are you going to do about that and how are you going to go about it?

We can best begin by going around the Octagon, with examples. The question to ask yourself, as you read these utterances, is not "Do people ever say these things to me?" I'm sure they do. These are the kinds of verbal battery everyone, male or female, encounters in daily life. Instead, ask yourself whether they are utterances you would use in speaking to other people; that's what you need to find out.

- *Section A:* "If you *really* wanted me to get ahead, you'd make an effort to be polite to my friends, no matter what you think of them."

  "If you *really* wanted me to get through school, you wouldn't always be on my back about helping you around the house."

  "If you *really* cared anything about having a winning team, you wouldn't give me some phony excuse every time I call you for practice."

- *Section B:* "If you *really* appreciated what I'm trying

to do for you, you wouldn't *want* to lie around on the beach all the time when you should be working."

"If you *really* had any consideration for your mother, you wouldn't *want* to quit your job."

"If you *really* intended me to have a fair shake in this job, you wouldn't *want* to see me driving an old beat-up clunker like this."

- *Section C:* "Don't you even *care* if this place always looks like a tornado just went through?

  "Don't you even *care* if your driving is going to double our insurance premiums?"

  "Don't you even *care* if I don't get my fellowship just because you gave me one lousy C? Do you get a kick out of seeing me lose something I've worked for for four years, because of five lousy points on a test?"

- *Section D:* "Even a *woman* ought to know that unless I go to this conference I'm not going to be promoted. It's not exactly secret information."

  "Even a *seven*-year-old should be able to understand that money doesn't grow on trees."

  "Even a *music* major should be able to get through algebra without pestering his roommate all the time, it seems to me."

- *Section E:* "Everybody in this house understands why you're so impossible to get along with, darling—don't worry about it."

  "Everybody in this fraternity knows why

you always spend every party sitting all by yourself—and we sympathize. No kidding, we really do."

"Every student in this school understands perfectly why most of the people who enroll in your classes drop out in the first week, Dr. Jones."

- *Section F:* "A woman who cared anything at all about having a meaningful relationship with another person would realize that there has to be some give and take on *both* sides."

  "A boss who had any consideration at all for the welfare of the employees would stop and think what it's *like* to work in a place like this."

  "A person whose salary is paid by the taxpayers of this state should keep in mind that he is paid to *serve*, not to boss people around."

- *Section G:* "Why don't you ever act like other women?"

  "Why don't you ever consider the effect of the things you say on other people? Don't you ever listen to yourself?

  "Why are you always criticizing me for everything I do instead of taking a good look at your *own* behavior? Answer me that!"

- *Section H:* "*Some* men would never in a million years believe a story like that one you just told me, honey."

  "*Some* officers might be inclined to be a little hard on a driver who seemed to have trouble staying in her own lane."

> "*Some* fathers might find it a little hard to understand why a kid big enough to have a driver's license can't find his way out to the trash, you know?"

Well—is that you talking? And if it is, do you care? (Please notice that I am Leveling. I am not saying, "Don't you even *care?*" I'm just asking.) If you don't care, the issue is closed, and that is your business, not mine.

Assume that you do care, on the other hand. You've read a lot of pages on how to defend yourself against other people who say these things to you. Let's concentrate now on how you *stop* if it's the other way around. How do you throw out all those patterns of speech that have been part of your personality for so long? And how do you do it without creating havoc in your life?"

One thing that won't help at all is to keep the same patterns, with the same stresses, and throw in little verbal lovepats to soften the blows. That's hitting somebody with a stick and then kissing the bruise to make it better. For example:

> "Sweetheart, you know I wouldn't hurt your feelings for anything in the world—you know how much I love you—but if you *really* wanted me to get through school, you wouldn't always be on my back about helping around the house."

That is no improvement. It may confuse the woman you're speaking to, since with the sloppy stuff at the beginning it's even harder for her to figure out why she feels like killing you when you're being so *nice*. That makes it worse, not better.

Another thing that won't help is tacking a cancellation clause on the end of your remarks. First the utterance, then "and if that sounds like I'm trying to be mean or something, I want you to know that I don't mean it that way." This becomes incredibly obvious after the second or third time.

I have a radical suggestion to make instead. Just make up your mind that you will eliminate the patterns on the Octagon from your speech. Not overnight; that's impossible. You're trying to break habits you've built up over years. Not without forgetting and having to start over many, many times. You are allowed to be human. What matters is for you to decide that those eight types of utterance are going to be absent from your speech from now on, and mean it. Every time you hear yourself use one, *notice* it; pay attention to your speech. If you've been doing this twenty times a day and in the first month you cut that down to sixteen times, that's progress. You have your whole life in which to make the change. If you were able to make it overnight, as a matter of fact, you'd probably scare everyone who knows you. They'd think you were coming down with something, slipping into nervous collapse, or concealing some awful secret. The fact that the process of change will inevitably be gradual is a piece of accidental good fortune; be grateful for it.

Use your Journal. Take every one of those examples from the Octagon; assume that you want to get across the message they contain but that you want to do it without verbal abuse; and work on them until you've found a satisfactory new way of saying that chunk of meaning. For example, from Section H:

> "Son, you know, I'm having a hard time understanding something. You have a driver's license, and you use my car. I understand that. I pay for the gas and the insurance, and I understand that, too. But when I ask you to take the trash out, I don't get any results. The two things don't fit together in my head very well. How about explaining it to me?"

This is Leveling, and it should work. Just be sure you don't add any Popular Wisdom to it along the lines of: "After all, if you expect to be granted privileges, you have to realize that with every privilege there also comes a responsibility." Your son has heard that until the first two or three words are enough to make him throw up, and it will immediately cancel any possibility of his discussing the chores problem with you. Depending on his age and patience, you will get one of the following back:

- "Aw, Dad, you're always on my back."
- "I don't know. I guess I'm just a creep. Okay?"
- "All right, I won't drive your car anymore. Okay?"
- "Maybe when I grow up I'll understand."

While you're throwing things out of your verbal-behavior chest, you might also throw out all the platitudes. They're useful only if you use them about once every three years, and in a situation for which they are the one and only perfect response. If you use them all the time, you may find them hard to give up, and I have a helpful trick for that. If I knew where I learned it, I would credit its author, but I first heard it years and years ago. It is a totally empty Popular Wisdom line that means nothing at all and goes like this:

> "You can't tell which way the train went by looking at the tracks."

As a verbal self-defense measure, this line is a useful response to anybody else's fatuous remarks. It usually provokes a long silence, and then—depending on the generation you're speaking to—either "You know, there may be a good deal of truth to that" or "That's *deep*." Every time you hear yourself say one of those platitudes, add to it—unless you're in a situation in which it would be dangerous to do so—"And furthermore, you can't tell which way the train went by looking at the tracks." This should break you of the platitudes because it will make you feel silly and draw your own attention to the habit.

I am taking it for granted that you have already thrown out all the obvious things such as yelling at people, swearing at them, and calling them names. No more "Look, stupid . . . " and "You idiot, why don't you look where you're going?" and all the way up the line to such elegant epithets as "Cretin! Pedant!" (Those are Academic Macho.) If you've been carrying on in this fashion, you have nothing to lose by giving it up, I assure you.

It will help to have somebody's aid in your project for change. Not somebody who'll jab you in the ribs every time and say, "Frank! You're doing it *again!*" in front of the whole world. Something more useful is needed, and more discreet.

As a young wife (a disgracefully young wife) I found myself suddenly dumped into a social milieu for which I was completely unprepared and in which I was absolutely terrified. What I did, in that state of terror, was adopt a manner that was so arrogant and so phony (complete, as I recall, with a phony British accent) that everyone thought I was intolerable. This did achieve one of my goals, which was to keep them away from me and let me huddle in a corner in peace; but it wasn't a very productive strategy for me as a person, and it embarrassed my husband.

We worked out something that helped a little. The moment he noticed me starting that behavior pattern or heard that phony accent, he would say something to me very softly—but he would call me "Margaret." It didn't embarrass me, and nobody else heard it, but it made me aware of what I was doing. Some evenings I was called "Margaret" as many as fifty times. If you have a trustworthy

"Significant Other" available at home, office, school, factory, or somewhere else convenient, work out an unobtrusive signal of that kind for them to use. It will help.

It will be obvious to you that your goal, particularly in those situations in which you are the *dominant* person in the conversation, is to switch to Leveler Mode whenever possible. Much of the time it will be neither safe nor possible, because you will be swimming among the sharks like everybody else. But it is essential that you always be able to work out what the Leveler *equivalent* for an utterance would be if your situation allowed you to use it. Rewriting all those examples at the beginning of this chapter in Leveler Mode is an excellent way to acquire this competence.

And I promise you, if you do no more than throw out the eight verbal patterns from the Octagon, the yelling and name calling, and the Popular Wisdom platitudes, you will have decreased the amount of verbal violence in your speech by a tremendous amount. That is genuine progress, and something to be proud of. One of the effects it will have is that, to your amazement, other people around you will stop being so irritating all the time. (This is of course partly a matter of your perceptions and partly a matter of theirs.) You are using verbal self-defense strategies when you are not the dominant speaker, and eliminating the abusive techniques when you *are*, and there is no way that those two factors in combination can fail to lower the tension in your verbal confrontations by about 50 percent. You'll run into people for whom it will do no good at all; that's inevitable. But let's not underestimate the value of a 50 percent improvement.

Last stop on the line is Guilt Station. What do you do about the problem of guilt? I have no instant solutions, and no tricks here. I can tell you things you must not do. For instance, you mustn't sit and go on and on to either yourself or others about what a monster you have been.

That is useless and boring, and soon people will either start avoiding you or agreeing with you. On the other hand, if you really need to talk about this, if you wake up every morning with the problem on your mind and a session or two with a tolerant friend doesn't help, don't ignore that. Go to someone who knows how to deal with such problems (by which I do not necessarily mean your friendly neighborhood eighty-dollars-an-hour psychotherapist). If you are a student, see a counselor. See a minister or a priest or a rabbi. Go to a crisis center or call a hotline. But don't ignore it. That much guilt you should not be feeling, not once you've realized what the problem is and begun working to change it. The time twenty years ago when you called the handicapped child in your second-grade class "Creepy Crip" should not be haunting you now.

A certain amount of guilt is normal and has to be lived with and worked through. If you had been hitting people with a baseball bat all unawares and were suddenly made to realize what you'd been doing and were persuaded to stop it, you would feel guilty. If you *didn't* feel that way, that would be worrisome. As pain comes along to tell you to keep your finger off that hot stove, guilt comes along to remind you not to whack other people, physically or verbally. Expect it, deal with it, and do the best you can. That's all anyone has the right to ask of you.

SUGGESTED READINGS

SIMPSON, TONY. "Real Men, Short Hair." *Texas Coach,* May 1973; also in *Intellectual Digest,* November 1973, pp. 76–78 (slightly abridged). (One of the best brief examples I know of the demand for masculinity at its stereotyped extreme.)

SONTAG, SUSAN. "The Double Standard of Aging." *Saturday Review,* September 23, 1972, pp. 29–38.

Special Chapter

For Women

17

If you are a woman who is given to being a verbal abuser, or if you cannot be sure whether that is true of you, the first thing for you to do is read Chapter Sixteen, the special chapter for men, and adapt it to your needs. (The differences are trivial; for example, you are perhaps less likely to swear at people than your male counterpart is.) If you are not in that situation, however, stay with me.

The two basic problems which you are now facing, unless you are very unusual, are these: (a) realizing that you are the victim of verbal abuse when that is in fact the case; and (b) dealing with the guilt you feel when you defend yourself. Both are tied inextricably to your image of yourself as a woman, and for a superb discussion of this I urge you to read the article by Susan Sontag listed in the suggested readings at the end of this chapter.

People do abuse you verbally. It happens a lot. It is expected to happen and considered to be the normal state of affairs. I am repeating myself only because I know what I am up against here—the weight of as many years of intensive cultural conditioning as your personal age at this reading.

How did you get this way? How, precisely, did you—a woman of intelligence and common sense—acquire the sort of mentality that makes you not only unaware that you are being mistreated but grateful for the mistreatment and bitterly angry with anyone who tries to take your part against your abuser?

It begins in infancy. You are "Daddy's little sweetheart" and "Mommy's darling little baby girl." It goes with the nursery rhymes and the picture books, where the princes and pirates and even the little boys go off to sea and derring-do, while the women sit on cushions and sew fine seams and live upon strawberries, sugar, and cream. It goes with falling down and being picked up and cuddled, while you see your brother told sternly in the same situation that boys don't cry. It follows you into your basic readers, in which all nurses and teachers and secretaries are female, and professors and truck drivers and executives and *important people doing important work* are male. In your spelling book the consonants are male, and they are reliable. The vowels are female, they can't be counted on for anything, and they get kicked around by the consonants.

It follows you through high school, where the boys play games while you cheer and twirl your baton. It accompanies you to church, where anything divine is male, and one gathers generically in *fellow*ship while wishing goodwill to all *man*kind. It follows you into marriage, where you are "the little woman" and frequently "the little mother." (Any current issue of *Modern Bride* would provide you with interesting examples here if you happen to be of the opinon that the rose-covered cottage and the rose-covered bride no longer exist.) You see a pair of books on the stands: One is called *How to Pick Up Men,* while its "companion" volume is *How to Pick Up Girls.*

The housewives on your television set are fascinated with the insides of their toilet bowls and the choice of one laxative over another. In committee meetings, it is taken for granted that you will take the notes and pour the coffee. If you have a secretary and treat her as secretaries are customarily treated by male bosses, you will not keep her two weeks—because you are "abrasive." The men you work with wear the same suit every day of the week and, for all you can tell, the same white shirt and the same pair of shoes—so long as the tie changes thrice weekly, they've done their duty. Try that yourself and you are "letting yourself go." Show any human frailty and you are "acting like a woman, which is repulsive"; show no human frailty and you are "acting like a man, which is repulsive in a woman."

Manage a career and a home and your children and keep yourself "well preserved," and you will be admired. Let any of that get to you and you will find that it's well known that women are always sick, always emotional, and usually hysterical. You may expect the man in your household to mow the lawn, but do not *ever* ask that dirty diapers be changed, that vomit be cleaned up, that cabinets be cleaned out and straightened, or that toilets be cleaned. Anticipate hearing from males in your house, as you return from work, that they have perhaps done the laundry "for you."

Nor will this improve as you grow older and become a "dear old thing." If you outlive your husband, you will be expected to miss him. You are expected to miss the children who demand of you a continual state of subservience. The cartoon strips in which elderly mothers are abused by loutish sons are supposed to make you laugh. When you are all alone, and could at last do something you want to do, you are expected to grieve over your "empty nest." If it was always empty, you will have been pitied all your life and you will die pitied. Nothing is more repulsive than a really old woman; she will be hidden away in a rest home unless she is poor, in which case she may become a "shopping-bag lady."

If you have a Ph.D., in no matter how prestigious a field, and you go into a hospital, expect the nurses and the doctors to refuse steadfastly to address you as "Doctor." (I assume that this may not apply if you are a "real" doctor—that is, if your degree is in medicine.) Expect your own doctor to call you by your first name (or "Miss/Mrs.") regardless of your professional status. Know that a wizard is glamorous and wondrous and awesome, and that a witch is an ugly, wicked old hag to be relentlessly hated.

Enough? I do certainly hope so, because I am beginning to bore myself. But it is the awful truth, and I rather expect it will remain the awful truth no matter how many Equal Rights Amendments may be passed. And I am surrounded by women who are convinced that they are totally free of any effect from all this cultural conditioning.

I am not referring just to the woman who did not finish high school, has perhaps never held a job outside her home, has raised three hulking sons who still bring her all their laundry to do, and is now a widow on Social Security. I am also speaking of women who consider themselves liberated, have advanced degrees, are successful in professions and trades ordinarily considered the province of men, and have never, for all I know, even seen an issue of *Modern Bride*.

Let us suppose that such a woman has been told by a male friend that he may call her this weekend and they might then go somewhere. Let us suppose that such a woman had already made plans to go that weekend to a conference which would be useful to her in her career, at which she would enjoy herself, and for which she has already paid. Who will sit home all that weekend by the phone, on the off chance that it will ring? Quite right, she will. And the fact that, when he does not call, she greets him on Monday morning with a thoroughly assertive "You bastard!" does not in any way differentiate her from that elderly widow I just mentioned. A braless woman sitting at the wheel of a two-ton semi, thinking to herself as she maneuvers that truck skillfully down the highway, "Oh, lord, will he call?" is not liberated. She has just been given different toys to play with.

It is a rather well-kept secret that most males in this country are delighted when women are sufficiently involved in some project, such as the ERA, that it is possible to keep them busy with that and keep their noses out of what is really happening. The longer such a project can be made to drag on, the longer it can be expected to serve as a distraction and "keep the ladies out of trouble." If it gives those same ladies the feeling that they are striking effective blows for their sex, so much the better. Unfortunately, ugly as they are, the true mechanisms that maintain the position of women are not legal ones, but linguistic ones.

It is a source of never-ending amazement to me that when I devote a day or two in my linguistics courses to verbal self-defense each and every academic term, the males in the room never open their mouths to object to anything I say. They do not have to. They lean back in their chairs and smile at me, politely, and we wait for what we know will happen; and it always does:—the female students defend them. Passionately. There may, they declare, be some men such as I describe, but not *their* father, brother, boyfriend, husband, dentist, lawyer, mechanic, and so on. They will willingly sit and hear me say that other women attack them verbally, and they will remember incidents in which their mother or sister or female friend turned on them with one of the Octagon attacks. But they claim staunchly that men who do those things are very rare and that even those who do them don't know they are doing anything of the kind and therefore can't be criticized for it. The only exceptions will be the militant feminists in the room, who will deny that *women* ever do such things.

What is to be done about all this? *Listen. Pay attention.* Are you or are you not being subjected to verbal abuse? One time around the Octagon, with examples, may help; do people say things like the following to you with the stresses indicated?

- *Section A:* "If you *really* cared anything about my feelings, you wouldn't embarrass me in front of my family by saying things like that."

  "If you *really* wanted the kids to be healthy, you wouldn't let them have all that junk food."

  "If you *really* had any interest in seeing the Women's Studies Department succeed, you'd come in and type mailing labels on Saturday like everybody else."

- *Section B:* "If you *really* understood the meaning of the simplest philosophical concepts, you wouldn't even *want* to join that group."

  "If you *really* loved me, you wouldn't *want* to take tennis lessons when you know I need the car."

"If you *really* were interested in a career, you'd go to secretarial school, where you belong."

● *Section C:* "Don't you even *care* if your mother is in there this minute crying her eyes out because you're breaking her heart?"

"Don't you even *care* if this company lost a major contract just because you refused to work overtime yesterday afternoon?"

"Don't you even *care* if your children's teeth all rot because you use that cheap toothpaste?"

● *Section D:* "Even a *woman* ought to be able to write a term paper that is at least comprehensible."

"Even someone with no more concern for the feelings of others than *you* have should be able to appreciate the fact that we can't always have everything we want in this life."

"Even a *woman* lawyer should be able to understand that a judge is entitled to be treated with respect in his own courtroom."

● *Section E:* "Every nurse on the floor knows what your problem is, dear—don't you worry about it."

"Every member of this club knows why you feel obliged to make us all look foolish with your ridiculous behavior, and we forgive you."

"Everyone understands, sweetheart, that when a woman reaches a certain age, she just isn't really herself. Indulging you is our pleasure, believe me."

- *Section F:* "A woman who expects to be treated with respect should learn that only *ladies* are accorded that sort of treatment."

  "A woman whose greatest pleasure in life is causing trouble and alienating people should not be surprised when they grow tired of tolerating her eccentricities."

  "A woman who can't even balance her own checkbook would probably be better off keeping her mouth shut about insurance policy choices, it seems to me."

- *Section G:* "Why don't you even *try* to do something about the way that child plays her stereo? We have to *live* in this neighborhood, you know."

  "Why don't you ever pay attention to the instructions I give in class for doing the homework?"

  "Why don't you ever make something different to eat for a change, sweetheart? I mean, there are only just so many ways a person can eat hamburger."

- *Section H:* "*Some* men would find it a little hard to understand why a woman who's capable of running her own business can't even get a meal on the table before nine o'clock."

  "*Some* kids would think it was pretty weird if their mother wouldn't go to the PTA picnic."

  "*Some* people would think it was really strange if they asked to spend a couple of days with a friend and got turned down just because of a *thesis*."

If none of these patterns of speech are ever used against you, not in your personal relationships, not at school, not in your work, not anywhere, you have my unreserved admiration. You are clearly someone who "has charisma" in abundance.

The solution to the problem is not for you, as a woman, to quickly learn how to use all these Octagon patterns against women, men, children, and your reflection in the mirror. You are not trying to go from a situation in which you are described by everyone as a "nice lady" to one in which you are perceived as a poor excuse for a bullying man. This is all too often where assertiveness training seminars lead you. I am not criticizing such groups; they may be extremely valuable, even if they do no more than teach you to say no once in a while. But there is a great potential for distortion here, and I would like to try to take you through it logically if I can.

Take as a given that men are brought up to be verbally abusive, usually without conscious awareness of that fact. Take as a second given that women don't approve of that and think it should be stopped. What conceivable sense does it make, then—with those first two premises in mind—to train *women* to behave in a way that it has already been agreed is indefensible in a man? If a swearing, yelling, swaggering man is an offense to the eye and ear, what is the excuse for a swearing, yelling, swaggering woman?

Even if it were possible for women to upset the political, economic, religious, and bureaucratic foundations of this country and to take over the present position held by men, what would have been accomplished if the result were only an exchange of roles, with women as the abusing group? The point of liberating women, it seems to me, must be to produce a better state of affairs, not a mirror image of the one now being objected to.

Verbal self-defense, as taught in this book, and practiced as carefully and as thoroughly as your ballet or your running or your harpsichord—plus the scrupulous elimination from your own verbal behavior of the patterns on the Octagon—should produce not a poor imitation of an abusive male but a truly self-confident woman.

The second question—how do you handle the guilt?—is not easy to answer. It will be much harder for you than for a man, because cultural specifications for women focus on service, dedication, and never making waves. If it is more than you can manage by yourself, seek out expert assistance from a counselor or religious adviser. In any case, know that it will come, and be prepared to work your way through it. All your life you have been trained in the ideas that (a) if anything goes wrong, it is your fault; and (b) it is your duty in life to see that nothing ever goes wrong. To realize that you have not been a nice lady, but have defended yourself and perhaps done so in a way that will be remembered, may turn out to be a heavier burden than you anticipated.

A situation that I encounter frequently is this one: A woman finds herself in a verbal confrontation with a man and, for once, defends herself. Then she goes home, and the guilt begins. For hours she torments herself, thinking how she must have *hurt* this man, what wounds she must have inflicted, how cruel she was, and so on. At last, when she can stand it no longer, she calls him up and confesses how sorry she is to have said such awful things to him. Whereupon he says: "Huh? What did you *say?*" He doesn't remember, you see. He will have assumed that she was playing the same game he was, and unless she went beyond self-defense and launched some truly nasty counterattack, he will have forgotten the whole episode in thirty seconds. The woman has now made a fool of herself by apologizing to this person for causing him pain when he was in no pain whatsoever. And she will pay for that in various ways, most of them self-inflicted.

Verbal self-defense is a gentle art. Even a *nice* lady is allowed to use it.

There are three traps I want to warn you not to fall into, by way of tying up this chapter. One is the Women's-Language Trap; one is the Wonder Woman Trap; and the last is the Circular "I Can't Win" Trap. The first is minor, but the other two are grave and ever-present dangers.

THE WOMEN'S-LANGUAGE TRAP

Recently there has been much research by both linguists and other social scientists on patterns of language associated with the sex of the speaker of English. Some basic references from this work are listed at the end of this chapter. This research has turned up some proposed characteristics of "women's speech" that are claimed to be absent from "men's speech," including the following:

1. intensives such as "very," "extremely," "really," "terribly," "awfully"
2. tag questions, such as "I should leave, shouldn't I?" and "That's too loud, isn't it?"
3. specialized vocabulary such as "mauve," "dear little X," "teeny-weeny," "simply darling," "chatter"
4. never being allowed to finish sentences, because of the toleration of constant interruption

This research is worthwhile and should certainly be pursued. Some cautions are necessary, however; and because it will be some time before they trickle down from the scholarly journals into the general media, I would like to make them here.

First, intonation is crucial to these alleged characteristics. I have heard very strong, masculine, thoroughly *male* males (in the stereotypical sense of all those terms) use every item on the women's-language list, including "teeny-weeny," without being perceived as effeminate or odd. There is a vast difference between saying "Mary is a simply darling person, and I enjoy being with her," and saying "Mary is a simply *darling* person, and I just *love* to be with her!"

Second, I have a strong suspicion that the reason women are so much more often heard using these items in mixed groups than the men they are being compared with is that the characteristics listed are representative of *subordinate* individuals. Since women are more frequently the subordinates in almost any mixed group, the statistics that come out of the research will tend to support the hypothesis. A clear distinction has to be made between phenomena of this kind and a situation such as one finds in Lakhota Sioux, in which a woman asking a question must use a different word to mark the sentence than a man does, otherwise the sentence itself is ungrammatical. For an American man to say, "What a *dear* little doily!" may be strange, but the man has not violated a rule of grammar in the sense of the Sioux example.

If the "women's language" hypothesis for English is taken too seriously at this early stage—which is something not intended by the researchers, I am sure—there may be a tendency for women to try to cut out of their speech the "female" characteristics, on an arbitrary basis. The idea is that this will cause them to be perceived as less subordinate, more confident, more competent, and so on. The results of such attempts, when I have sat and watched them, have almost without exception been either embarrassing or ridiculous. You have only to imagine a woman who is determined to interrupt as frequently as possible, rather than allow herself to be interrupted, while the dominant individuals in the confrontation continue to try to do their usual quota of interrupting, in order to imagine the chaos to which this can lead.

Until this research has been carried considerably farther, I have a suggestion. If your skirt is mauve, and you know it is, don't be afraid to say so. "Hell, I don't know what damned color the fool thing is!" doesn't sound assertive; it sounds absurd.

THE WONDER WOMAN TRAP

In almost any Network on which you find yourself, there will be an opportunity to fall into this trap. It goes as follows. Most of the members of the network are male, and all of them already have a certain amount of status. You, the woman, enter this group, and it is made clear to you that directly ahead of you—and determining your eventual status—is a set of hurdles. The hurdles may be salary steps or tenure review or a probationary year. A position at a fast-food place will offer precisely the same sort of hurdles as one at the most prestigious place of employment, but the labels may differ.

Because you are eager to jump the hurdles and move up the network in status, you accept with gratitude all sorts of small duties and assignments that are offered you. They will be presented as opportunities, things that the higher-status seniors present would like to do themselves but are willing to pass on to you because they want to see you get ahead.

And then one day, six months or a year later, you will wake up one morning and realize that—whatever the network—you are doing vast amounts of work, much of it dreary detail work that nobody enjoys doing. Furthermore, you are buried in an impossible schedule that endangers both your health and your sanity, and there is no sign of any end to it. Every new dreary task is passed on to you because (a) the precedent has been set; (b) you are clearly so *good* at all these things and so delighted to do them; and (c) you fell for it.

This ancient ploy began in the home and still continues there, where Dad invites twenty people for dinner without asking the "little woman" first because, he will be happy to tell you, there is nothing she loves more than getting out there in the kitchen and cooking for a bunch of people. And boy, can she cook! Little boys learn the routine well before puberty, when they are discovered to be incapable of doing the dishes—they break them and put spoons down the garbage disposal—but their sister is very good at dishes and doesn't mind doing them.

Do try not to fall for this one. You can be sure that the credit for the magnificent way you handle everything piled upon you, as well as your "input" to statements of all kinds that issue forth from your unit, will go not to you but to the organization inside which you are busily playing Wonder Woman. If you don't notice, you'll spend the rest of your life like that. And when you finally have to be dispensed with, it will be acknowledged that heaven only knows how they will get along without you—but it will be too late.

Getting out of this trap if you are already in it is a matter requiring careful planning and advanced skills. The most useful clue I can give you is to get out your Network Diagram and take a long, hard look at it—from your central position as Wonder Woman, who can *always* take on just one more task and manage it somehow. If an escape route exists, that is where you will find it. Certainly, you can prevent the situation from escalating. The next time you are approached with a new little plum, you can say that you're sorry, but you can't take that one on. And stick to that.

And by the way, spotting a new incoming female on whom you can dump your burden before *she* catches on is not an ethical solution, however tempting it may be.

THE CIRCULAR "I CAN'T WIN" TRAP

This last one, like the Wonder Woman Trap, comes out of the cultural conditioning of women. But it has in it a heavy interlarding from a kind of instant feminism. It turns up in women who have read one feminist book or three issues of *Ms. Magazine* or taken one women's studies course and have nothing like an understanding of the issues. And it goes like this:

> "Because I am a woman, nothing I do has any chance of succeeding, so there's no point in my even trying to do anything—but it's not my fault; and it's not because I couldn't be a great writer or judge or engineer or scientist or anything I want to be—it's because I'm a woman, and nothing I do has any chance of succeeding."

That will go around and around forever, and it will provide you with an excuse to do nothing for the rest of your life. You can use it as an excuse not to take an exam, an excuse not to cook dinner, an excuse not to apply for a job, an excuse not to take a statistics course, an excuse for *anything.*

It can serve as an excuse for always putting forth the minimum effort possible and as a reason for every failure you have. And it is utterly phony. While it is true that it is harder for a woman to succeed in most areas involving prestige and power, it is not impossible. It may take more work than would have been demanded of a man. If you don't choose to put forth that additional effort, fine. If you want to claim that it's unfair that it should be required of you, that's also fine. I agree with you. But be honest with yourself. When you write a shoddy paper and it comes back with a D on it, it probably has that D because it is a shoddy paper, not because you are female. It may be that the same shoddy paper from a male student would have had a C on it. That's possible. But if you do A work, and do it consistently, you will eventually get your A's.

Don't let this become a kind of permanent crutch that you lean on. It will only turn you into a bitter, crippled person, and you don't need it. Learn to defend yourself instead.

REFERENCES AND SUGGESTED READINGS

Books:

LAKOFF, ROBIN. *Language and Woman's Place.* New York: Harper & Row, Publishers, Inc., 1975. (This brief book is one of the landmark publications in research on the characteristics of female speech behavior.)

MILLER, CASEY, and KATE SWIFT. *Words and Women: New Language in New Times.* New York: Anchor Books, 1977.

RUETHER, ROSEMARY, ed. *Religion and Sexism.* New York: Simon & Schuster, Inc., 1974. (This collection of articles takes up the religious and ethical sources of sexism, with much useful material on linguistic phenomena.)

Articles:

FLORMAN, SAMUEL C. "Engineering and the Female Mind:

Why Women Will Not Become Engineers." *Harper's,* February 1978, pp. 57–63.

KRAMER, CHERIS; BARRIE THORNE; and NANCY HENLEY. "*Perspectives on Language and Communication.*" *Signs* 3, no. 31 (Spring 1978): 638–51. (This article may be difficult to find. However, it is a painstaking review of the various research studies into sex differences in communication and well worth seeking out. Highly recommended.)

"The New Housewife Blues." *Time,* March 14, 1977, pp. 61–69.

PARLEE, MARY BROWN. "Women Smile Less for Success." *Psychology Today,* March 1979, p. 16. (A discussion of male-female nonverbal behavior and its effect on perception of status.)

RICHMOND-ABBOTT, MARIE, and NADEAN BISHOP. "The New Old-Fashioned Womanhood." *Human Behavior,* April 1977, pp. 62–69. (A careful discussion of the various systems now proposed for training women to center their lives around home and family. Highly recommended.)

SONTAG, SUSAN. "The Double Standard of Aging." *Saturday Review,* September 23, 1972, pp. 29–38. (This article carefully analyzes the problems of self-image in both men and women and traces the development of such problems through various stages of life. I cannot recommend it too highly.)

WILLS, GARY. "Feminists and Other Useful Fanatics." *Harper's,* June 1976, pp. 35–42.

Conclusion

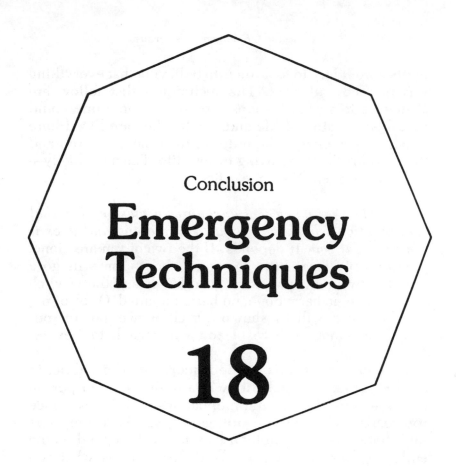

Emergency Techniques

18

This final chapter is a collection of techniques to be used in genuine emergency situations. With any luck, you'll never encounter most of them; but one or two are bound to come your way. I want to make it clear that what I offer you here are only stopgap measures, and that some of the emergencies are more dire than others. You should not, therefore, look upon the suggestions I make as fail-safe techniques. They are nothing of the kind.

If a surgeon tried to tell you over the phone how to do an emergency appendectomy or a flight controller tried to talk you down at the controls of an airplane when the pilot had collapsed and you knew nothing about flying, neither would try to fool you into believing that everything was perfectly all right. The techniques that follow are analogous to such situations, except that only one could be called a matter of life and death. They are listed here in what I perceive as the order of their danger to you and their likelihood of occurring in your life. The most likely—and least dangerous—appear first.

What to do when you encounter a master of verbal manipulation who knows what you're doing and does it right back at you. It depends. If the two of you are alone, you probably have little to worry about. You will go a round or two, perhaps have a good laugh, and then switch to Leveling; no harm done, no harm intended. Or else you, as a beginner, will be shown a trick or two, put in your place, and *then* the two of you will switch to Leveler Mode.

Unfortunately, this happens more often in public, in situations that may make it awkward for the other person to follow his or her natural inclinations. In this case, once you realize what you are up against, you have only one safe strategy—and even then its safety will depend on the ethics of your opponent. Nevertheless, this is what you must do: Rely on the expert to get both of you out of it safely. Go to Computer Mode, pay close attention to the clues the expert feeds you, don't betray by word or movement or expression any amazement you may feel at things that happen as the situation develops, and trust the expert's superior skill. Any attempt you make to "help" is likely to make it impossible for him or her to carry out the necessary moves. Don't just do something, *sit* there.

I suffered a lot of unnecessary knocking about as a beginner before I realized at last that my attempts to help the expert present were only creating problems and making things worse. I learned the hard way and would like to save you that.

How to handle an angry group. All the confrontations described in this beginner's manual have had to do with you as novice versus one or perhaps two or three other people. It does sometimes happen that you must face a really furious *group* of people, perhaps quite a large group. For instance, as a teacher you may have to face a room full of angry students or angry parents. As a speaker, you may have to face an outraged audience. As the president of any organization, you may have to face a group of angry members.

First, let the group exhaust its anger if you can. (This rule often applies to angry single individuals who outrank you markedly in status as well, by the way.) You can take quite a lot of verbal garbage—the equivalent of thrown tomatoes and lemon pies—without allowing it to destroy your calm, if you make up your mind to do that. It must not be allowed to go on forever. And it must not be allowed to go on if it becomes clear that it is only feeding the flames. But in most cases, letting half a dozen people stand up in your audience and tell you what a mess you are and in how many ways you are that kind of mess, while you listen in polite and neutral silence, will lower the tension in the room and make everyone more willing to be reasonable. (Note: If professional agitators are involved, this *won't* help. Beginners have no business dealing with professional agitators and hecklers, just as those who can swim only three laps have no business trying a swim across the English Channel. If this is what you face, *leave* and let the audience and the pros work it out for themselves. That is the only sensible action for you to take.)

When the half-dozen representatives of the group's anger have been heard and you have exhibited your willingness to let all sides of the question be aired, the next step is to behave precisely as if the group you face were only one person. This is not as strange as it may seem, since by this time a mob personality will usually have developed. It will be a Blamer Mob, a Placater Mob, or some other type. The only difference between such a mob and an individual is the ease with which the mob can be led—and the question is only whether you are going to lead it or whether somebody else is. Use everything you know about being charismatic. If things begin to heat up in spite of your efforts, switch to Computer Mode and be just as meaningless and abstract as you possibly can be.

Above all, don't lose your temper or show any sign that you are distressed. An expert can Level with an angry group and get away with it, but novices are trampled into the earth that way. Don't try it, unless it simply appeals to you as an experiment and you are willing to trade the consequences for the experience.

How to handle a Sitting Duck. Every now and then you will be faced with a moral dilemma—an *ethical* emergency. Somewhere in one of your Interaction Networks, at either your own level or slightly above it, there will be a pathetic example of someone you could easily take apart and make a pale gray smear of, verbally. Furthermore, this person will persist in begging to be treated that way. He or she will continually carry out what Sitting Duck perceives as strikingly clever verbal moves against you and will wait confidently for you to come back with *your* move and be carried away bleeding.

Once you spot this person, you have only once choice, and it isn't pleasant. *Ignore* Sitting Duck. There is no honor, no victory, and no decency, in using your superior strength and skill against someone of this kind, and you must not stoop to it no matter how strong the temptation. Maintain Computer Mode, never lose your temper, and wait. In time, the Sitting Duck will destroy itself, and it will be remembered that you never deviated from the proper ethical position. (By "in time," I really mean "in time." It may take years, during which you will take a lot of heat and listen to many unpleasant words. If you don't care for this, take Harry S. Truman's advice and get out of the kitchen if the heat is too much for you.)

You will frequently be challenged by other people, who will call what you are doing cowardice or hypocrisy or professional suicide or accuse you of "being a martyr," and other similar epithets. Some of these people will be well-meaning friends, and some will be pretending to be well-meaning friends; it makes no difference. You look them calmly in the eye, you inform them that you haven't the slightest idea what they are talking about, and you stick to that position. It is cheap to use your skills against people who cannot defend themselves against you when it is you personally that they are attacking. Don't stoop to that, and the day will come when you'll be very glad you didn't.

How to handle the total communication breakdown. Sometimes, nothing works. You say something, making the proper move specified in your manual, and nothing happens. You get an icy silence, a blank look, folded arms. You try another move—you try Leveling, perhaps. And still nothing happens.

What this means is that you are lacking some vital piece of information. You have broken a rule you know nothing about, perhaps because the other person is from a different cultural group than you are, perhaps for entirely personal reasons.

In this situation you have only one appropriate response. You become absolutely silent, too. And you wait. Somebody will break eventually and either say something or leave. You can hope that the somebody will not be you or that the other person will offer you the missing information you need. If not, please remember—you cannot win them all.

If this happens to you in a situation in which you are

facing a group and you have a responsibility to fulfill—for example, you are there to try to convince management that your union is entitled to a wage increase, or you are there to try to convince a faculty committee that a change should be made in an academic requirement—be sure that you make your position clear before you resort to silence. Say, unambiguously, "What I'm here for is to talk about a wage increase. I'm willing to listen to what you have to say and I'm willing to enter into a discussion. If you don't want to say anything, I'm also willing to wait." *Then* sit back and say nothing more. It's their move.

Reverse-signal technique. What on earth do you do, as a beginner, if you must represent a position with which you disagree and you dare not refuse to do so?

This happens. In this real world, where people have families to feed and jobs to hold down and all sorts of legitimate pressures and threats hanging over them, this happens. Pretending that it does not, or that most people are capable of being saints and standing by their principles regardless of the cost, is absurd.

Assume that you are a student teacher and you have been told to convince the parents of your students that the book you've been ordered to use in your classroom is a good one, though you yourself think it is a dreadful book. If you say you won't use or defend the book, you'll flunk student teaching, you won't get your teaching credential, years of school at considerable sacrifice for your family and yourself will have been wasted, and somebody else will move in and defend the book as ordered. That person *will* pass student teaching, get the teaching certificate, and so on.

This is an awful moral dilemma, and I don't intend to hand down moral doctrine. Unlike the Sitting Duck situation, the issues are not clear-cut. I once compromised in a situation like this, long ago, because I had three small kids to feed. I despise myself for it to this day; but if I had it to do over again, I rather expect I would only do what I did then. It isn't fair—you should not be put in such a bind. But I assure you that when something unpleasant or unpopular must be transmitted to a group, it is frequently a task that nobody high on the power hierarchy will touch; thus, it is "delegated" down the line until it arrives at you. The question then becomes: In a situation where you feel you have no choice but to compromise your principles, is there any way you can do that without sacrificing the entire ball game?

Yes. There is a technique from espionage and advertising—a curious but much-related pair. It requires careful advance preparation but is certainly not beyond your skills.

Write down what it is that you are expected to say—the part where you defend the book you despise, for example. Then consider your audience. Think of everything you know about them, their likes and dislikes, and especially what words are likely to have a negative cultural loading for them. Make a list of those words (leaving out curses or ethnic slurs, of course.) Now go back to your speech and very carefully salt those words through it wherever you can. Your goal is to make the audience leave convinced that they have heard you speak *for* the book you hate—since that's the compromise you have been forced to—and prepared to claim that they heard you speak for it, but convinced that they hate that book. In other words, you have done your best and you have failed; that can happen to anyone.

Let me give you one concrete example. I don't expect to find myself in a position where I feel that I must face a group of angry students and argue for a particular curriculum change that I am in fact against. I don't think that's going to happen to me at this stage in my life. However, if it *did* happen, I would know what to do.

On my campus, which is a huge urban multicultural campus with only about ten thousand parking spaces for at least fifty thousand people with cars, the parking problem is a Unifying Metaphor to end all unifying metaphors. It is a rare day when any student does not have at least one negative incident in his or her life that is due entirely to the shortage of parking space (and the absence of adequate public transportation). I would therefore get up before the group of students and present the new curriculum change entirely in speech patterns having to do with being at the wheel of a car, successfully negotiating the highway, finding a secure place to park, and so forth. (This is frequently done with a "ship," "a safe berth," and "bringing (X) into port," but it takes little ingenuity to shift your vehicular vocabulary.) I would hammer away at the logical arguments *for* what I was against, since they are known to have little effect on the audience for any speech. And at the end the students would go out and vote down the change in curriculum. They would probably not realize that the source of their anger was my unrelenting reminders of the parking problem; and the superior who had forced me into that corner would not be able to say that I had not done my duty as ordered.

You might think that this could backfire on you, and I suppose it is possible. You could overdo it to such an extent that it would become parody—maybe. But you'd have to work at it. It is frequently this technique that is responsible for one astounding truth: Commercials that people claim they *hate* usually sell more of the product than the tasteful kind.

Spotting and dealing with the phony Leveler. Way

back at the beginning of this book I told you that there was probably nothing more dangerous than the phony Levelers. They tempt you—seduce you, actually—into a position of total vulnerability. Then, whap! And it's too late.

The most obvious clues to identifying these persons are the eight attacks on the Octagon, with the proper stresses present, but a quite different vocabulary. The phony Leveler will never come at you as any sort of overt menace. Here's a typical phony Leveler utterance:

> "If you *really* wanted to have a meaningful relationship, love, you would realize that it has to be based on a foundation of complete mutual trust."

And a few more . . .

- "Even someone as sensitive to others as *you* are should be able to realize how much it hurts me when you keep secrets from me."
- "*Some* people might think that because you refuse to take part in this discussion like the rest of us, you don't really want to be part of the group . . . you know what I mean?"
- "Look, I know you've probably been shafted so many times that you don't trust anybody anymore. Everybody *here*, including me, understands that, and sympathizes. We really do. But a person who wants to get beyond the past and do some genuine growing toward the future has got to be able to give up these old misconceptions."

Your tendency in response to such moves is to tell your secrets, lay bare your confidences, and *trust* the phony Leveler—often in front of other people. Then, when it is too late, you find out that that is just what it was all about, and now the phony has you right where he or she wants you. The phony Leveler will have a lot to say about how "paranoid" it is of you to be so "emotional, distrustful, unwilling to surrender your own preconceptions," and so on. Frankly, being frightened in a collapsing building is not paranoid; it is common sense. Being frightened when you have reason to think you have a phony Leveler after you is also common sense.

This is a situation in which it is better to be safe than sorry. If you hear the Octagon patterns and you have a funny feeling that things are not right, stay in Computer Mode until you are absolutely certain where you are. Nobody can hurt you more deeply, or more permanently, than a phony Leveler whose spiel you fell for out of innocence. You are entitled to refuse to risk that.

Verbal self-defense against physical violence. This is the last one, and perhaps the worst. Let us hope that you never encounter it. With all my heart I hope that you are never a teacher faced by a student who outweighs you by fifty pounds and has a knife at your throat, or a woman alone in a bedroom with a would-be rapist, or an elderly man facing a drunken punk in an alley. I can hope nothing like this ever happens to you, but I cannot guarantee it.

The attempt to counter physical violence with verbal defense techniques is definitely not recommended for beginners. But if you find yourself trapped and you must do *something,* here are my suggestions.

Go to Computer Mode and stay there. Most people determined on hurting you physically are more interested in seeing your fear and hearing you plead for mercy than they are in the act of violence itself. If you show no emotion and don't appear to be either frightened or arrogant, you will keep them from achieving that goal. This should win you some time, as they keep trying to get you to show the terror that they want to see. It may be enough time for someone to come to your aid. It may also convince them to find somebody who is more fun to abuse than you are.

Your goal is to keep the level of tension low, to keep your *attacker* from panicking—a major danger, however strange it may seem—and to win time. Be as absolutely neutral as you possibly can. Do not Blame. Do not Placate, whatever you do. Do not go to the Distracter Mode that betrays inner panic. Stay in Computer Mode, verbally and nonverbally.

In the hands of an expert, this will work. That is why experts are sent to negotiate with persons who have shut themselves up in buildings with hostages at gunpoint. That's why experts are sent to try to talk people down from ledges and bridge railings when they are determined on suicide. In a beginner's hands, it may fail, but it is worth a try. It is most assuredly safer than an attempt at physical violence, unless you number karate among your personal skills.

Do your very best to get your attacker involved in an abstract discussion of violence—not the particular altercation the two of you are involved in, but violence in general, all in Computer Mode. The longer you can keep the potentially violent person talking to you, the better your chances of coming out of it without serious injury.

I am convinced that unless you *are* an expert at one of the conventional martial arts, and totally capable of defending yourself in that way, this is much safer than the frequently recommended hatpins, bottles of spray chemicals, jabs to the eyes or the groin, and the like. If you make a mistake with one of *those,* you are not likely to get a second chance. Just *talking,* on the other hand, is less likely to be interpreted as an attack or to panic the violent person you are dealing with.

Good luck.

For information about the *Gentle Art of Verbal Self-Defense Newsletter* write to Suzette Haden Elgin, Route 4, Box 192E, Huntsville, Arkansas 72740

Index